CARFER
,9

D0592284

VGM Opportunities Series

OPPORTUNITIES IN **PARAMEDICAL CAREERS**

Alex Kacen

Revised by
Terence J. Sacks

Foreword by
Mark Lockhart
National Association of Emergency Medical Technicians

 **VGM Career Horizons**
NTC/Contemporary Publishing Group

HS ⁷⁄₀₁ 15.00

Library of Congress Cataloging-in-Publication Data
Kacen, Alex.
  Opportunities in paramedical careers / Alex Kacen ; revised by
Terence J. Sacks.
    p. cm. — (VGM opportunities series)
    Originally revised in 1994; this ed. provides updates.
    ISBN 0-8442-2906-7 (cloth). — ISBN 0-8442-2907-5 (pbk.)
    1. Allied health personnel—Vocational guidance—United States.
  2. Paramedical education—United States Directories. I. Sacks,
  Terrence J. II. Title. III. Series.
  R697.A4K32 1999
  610.69—dc21   99-26183
                                                      CIP

Cover photographs: © PhotoDisc, Inc.

Published by VGM Career Horizons
A division of NTC/Contemporary Publishing Group, Inc.
4255 West Touhy Avenue, Lincolnwood (Chicago), Illinois 60712-1975, U.S.A.
Copyright © 2000 by NTC/Contemporary Publishing Group, Inc.
Printed in the United States of America
International Standard Book Number: 0-8442-2906-7 (cloth)
                                                      0-8442-2907-5 (paper)
99 00 01 02 03 04 LB 18 17 16 15 14 13 12 11 10 9 8 7 6 5 4 3 2 1

CONTENTS

ABOUT THE AUTHOR

Dr. Kacen earned his Ed.D. degree from the University of Houston in 1973 with a major in career development—career-related testing, counseling, and education. His dissertation research was done in the Texas Medical Center (Houston) and investigated career opportunities in the health field. Before receiving his doctorate, he taught mathematics and foreign languages, his undergraduate and master's major fields. After completing his doctorate, he was a career education consultant for the state of Indiana and directed a college career testing and counseling service. Other professional activities have included serving as an external evaluator for the national career education program in Puerto Rico and developing original career-related assessment instruments used by schools, colleges, and workers representing many occupations. He has also been a member of the admissions committee of a displaced home-makers program. Dr. Kacen has published more than 25 articles on career development, including a book on career transitions among adults, a topic he has discussed as a featured guest on a five-part ABC television series. Dr. Kacen also acts as a management consultant to business firms—offering a wide variety of career- and employment-related workshops to such firms. He is currently the director of the Career Directions Center in San Antonio, Texas.

This edition was revised by Terry Sacks, a lifelong journalist and author specializing in health- and medicine-related topics.

FOREWORD

As a paramedic for more than fifteen years, I have seen my fair share of what life has to offer: from delivering a baby to telling the family of a seventy-nine-year-old cancer patient that their beloved mother and grandmother had died, I have been there. It is not an easy job—there is a physical and mental price that may be paid—but the rewards are truly outstanding. There are very few careers where you can do your job and know that you made the difference between pain and comfort, between sickness and health, between life and death.

Whether as an emergency medical technician-paramedic, nurse practitioner, or physical therapy assistant, if you are interested in a health career you need to have one very special characteristic: a genuine desire to help people. Coupled with compassion and a very deep respect for life, that desire grows and fosters wonderful opportunities for you to care for patients in need and to learn more about the miracle of life. Don't be surprised if you learn something about yourself along the way as well.

The subject of health-care reform has dominated the evening news and newspaper headlines in recent years. Through all of the discussions and arguments, only one thing is certain: health care and the ways it is provided will continue to change. The emphasis will be on providing quality health services for everyone. But how can we do that, when our existing system is already overtaxed as a result of AIDS, teen pregnancies, cancer, heart disease, and an epidemic of violence? A shortage of physicians and nurses further complicates an already treacherous situation. The answer, or at least a partial answer, may be contained in the pages of this book: the allied health professions. These trained and educated professionals can assist and supplement physicians and nurses in caring for the growing numbers of patients in need of basic health services. An expansion of the role and practice of these professionals could further improve the efficacy with which some health services are delivered. In some cases, that expansion is already being actively explored.

As you consider your career choice, look carefully and closely—not just at the choices in front of you, but at the qualities and desires within you. Only then will you know if you are making the right choice. And to those who will choose health care, welcome to the team!

> Mark Lockhart, NREMT-P
> Past President
> National Association of Emergency
>   Medical Technicians
>
> Coordinator
> Office of Paramedic Education
> Department of Emergency Medicine
> St. John's Mercy Medical Center
> St. Louis, MO

CHAPTER 1

PARAMEDICALS AND PARAPROFESSIONALS CLOSE-UP

It happened so quickly that Ted, a self-made businessman in his mid-fifties who ran a successful insurance agency, didn't know what hit him. He was at home relaxing on a sunny Sunday afternoon, preparing to barbecue some steaks, when suddenly he felt dizzy and was hit by a strange numbness of his right side, both arm and leg. He called out to his wife, Heather, who heard him and ran out of the house.

"What's the matter, dear?" she cried. "I don't know, but the whole right side of my body seems to be numb and I feel dizzy. Maybe I need a doctor," came Ted's reply.

Heather, whose best friend, Alice, had recently suffered a stroke, knew that Ted's symptoms resembled those of a stroke and that time was extremely important, in fact, that it could be a matter of life and death. So she immediately got on the phone and dialed 911, the emergency number.

When the operator answered, Heather told her what had happened and asked that they send an ambulance immediately. Within a few minutes she heard the ambulance wail, and shortly afterwards she admitted a two-man team of paramedics. Quickly, the two checked Ted's breathing, which was labored. They placed him deftly on a stretcher and positioned his head and shoulders on a

1

pillow to help him breathe a little easier. Placing him in the ambulance, they proceeded to the closest hospital. Once there a team of emergency workers rushed Ted into the ER, where he was quickly examined by the attending physician.

And it was a good thing that they had, for stroke is a very serious business. In fact, it is a killer, the number three cause of death in the United States (after heart attack and cancer), accounting for approximately 145,000 deaths a year.

The attending physician first performed an arteriography to determine both what kind of stroke Ted had and the proper treatment for it. The procedure located a blockage of the artery supplying blood to the brain, known in medical terminology as an *embolism.*

The doctor knew that since Ted had been rushed to the hospital in a matter of minutes, he was a good candidate for the administration of TPA, a so-called clodbuster, which has obtained wonderful results in opening up circulation to large areas of the brain before they can become permanently damaged.

A surgeon assistant was standing by in case an emergency carotid enderectomy had to be performed. (A surgeon assistant is neither a nurse nor a physician, but a medical worker a notch or two lower than a physician who can perform most of the procedures of the surgeon, under a surgeon's guidance.) Carotid enderectomy has proven effective in stroke patients who have at least 70 percent blockage of the carotid artery. In such cases the surgeon opens up the blocked artery and removes the plaque blocking it.

In Ted's case, the surgeon assistant, working under the attending surgeon, handled a variety of duties very much like those done by the surgeon, thus freeing up the surgeon in charge to take care of more complex duties.

After the surgery, Ted, as part of the treatment plan, received both occupational and physical therapy. In both cases, the physical therapist and the occupational therapist were helped by special assistants. The occupational therapist assistant helped Ted to relearn the tasks involved in caring for himself—such as putting on his shoes and shirt, buttoning his shirt, clasping and tying his tie, and, in general, grooming himself as he had been doing prior to the stroke.

Afterwards, Ted was referred to a physician assistant, when his own physician was out of town. The physician assistant, a very knowledgeable young man, looked and acted like a physician, and had he not introduced himself as "I'm Tom Trimble, a physician assistant, and I handle Dr. Phillips's patients when he is not around," Ted would never have known that he was not a doctor. But since Trimble had come right out and admitted that he was not a doctor, Ted could not help wondering what he had gotten himself into and why he could not see his own physician. However, his fears and concerns proved groundless as soon as he learned that not only was Trimble able to spend more time with him, he also was able to lay out a complete schedule of exercise, diet, and medication that would prove very helpful in speeding Ted's postoperative recovery over the weeks ahead.

In the case just described, we have gone into detail about a stroke suffered by a middle-aged businessman; his treatment by paramedics, otherwise known as emergency medical technicians, who were the first on the scene; his surgery in the hospital; and his postoperative recovery.

Although he didn't realize it, Ted was treated by many paramedicals during each stage of his illness: first by the paramedicals (or EMTs) in the ambulance; next by a nurse anesthetist, who worked in the hospital under the direction of the anesthesiologist (medical doctor) who placed him under anesthesia prior to surgery; then by a surgery assistant, who acted as an assistant first-class in working with the surgeon during every phase of the surgery and handling the stitching of the wound itself; then by the occupational and physical therapy assistants, who facilitated Ted's recovery and helped him regain the full use of his arms and legs; and finally by the physician assistant, in Ted's postsurgery follow-up visits.

Paramedicals, often referred to as *allied health paraprofessionals,* have been described by the American Medical Association as "a large cluster of health related personnel who fill necessary roles in the healthcare system."

These paramedical workers are in the fullest sense of the word, members of the medical team. They complement, extend, and otherwise support the work of doctors and other healthcare workers. As seen by the example above, they work with doctors, podiatrists, dentists, and physical and occupational therapists to make their jobs easier and more effective. At the same time, they are helping to relieve the critical shortage of healthcare workers by taking many of the more routine chores off of their shoulders, thus allowing our healthcare system to function more effectively.

In many cases paramedicals work in new career fields that have emerged only in the past twenty or twenty-five years, or in the case of the physician assistant (PA), in the past thirty-five years or so. They ordinarily work under the direct supervision of a physician, dentist, podiatrist, or occupational or physical therapist. When they do not work under a physician or other medical professional, as is true of many nurse practitioners or dental laboratory technicians, they almost always follow the orders of the doctor or other professionals involved. In so doing, they serve as extenders, or right-hand assistants, by enabling the doctor to render medical care or treatment to many more patients than would otherwise be possible.

PARAPROFESSIONALS DEFINED

What exactly is a paraprofessional? Most of us, for instance, know that a *professional* is one who by virtue of his or her education and training has acquired skills necessary for a given field. Medicine, engineering, law, accounting, and architecture are all fields that require professionally trained practitioners.

To qualify for such professions, you must have at least a bachelor's degree and, in many cases, considerably more education, as in the case of medicine. Here you must have at least four years of undergraduate (college) work, four years of medical school, and at least three years of residency (specialty) training, depending upon the field of medicine in which you choose to specialize.

Not so clear, however, is the meaning of the term *paraprofessional* or *paramedical*, for these terms are describing careers that have emerged only in the last twenty or twenty-five years. To be sure, many of us have heard these terms—paramedicals or paralegals—but few of us really understand their meanings, or our understanding is fragmentary and incomplete at best.

It will help to define the term *para,* the Greek word for "beside." The paramedical is, therefore, the one who works near or "beside" the physician, dentist, or optometrist. In the case of the physician assistant and nurse practitioner, not only do they work near the physician, they perform many of the same functions. They diagnose and treat patients, take case histories, perform physical examinations, and, in most cases, even prescribe medications.

For our purposes, we have classified paramedicals as all those whose work meets the following guidelines:

1. Usually, but not always, you must have completed a lengthy training program on the college level or equivalent. In some cases, you have the option of qualifying with only

a year of college education or equivalent experience, but in most cases the program will last at least three years.

2. The educational background required to qualify for the career closely resembles that of the profession to which it corresponds, except that it is shorter and of more limited duration. The training program of the physician assistant, for instance, is like that of the physician, except it is not as detailed, long, or comprehensive.

3. Paramedicals work under the supervision and guidance of the professionals they serve and to whom they are responsible. But the amount of responsibility you have will depend to a great extent on your education and experience and where you work. For example, in certain rural and outlying areas of the country, physician assistants may not see their supervising physician for a week or more at a time, but they are in constant touch with their supervisors by phone or computer.

A word of caution: Don't confuse *paramedical workers* with *paramedics.* The terms are not interchangeable. *Paramedics* are the emergency medical technicians. *Paramedicals,* on the other hand, are part of an array of health professionals who work near or beside and in support of other healthcare professionals.

Within the parameters listed above fall such careers as physician assistants, medical assistants (who work at another level completely from that of the physician assistant), nurse practitioners, nurse anesthetists, and nurse-midwives; ophthalmic medical assistants, technicians, and technologists; dental assistants, hygienists, and laboratory technicians; physical therapy assistants and occupational therapy assistants; podiatrist assistants; and several others, all of which will be fully described in this book.

OTHER HEALTHCARE WORKERS

Several other healthcare careers that might be considered allied health careers have not been included in this book because they require less training than that required in paramedical work. Included in this category are such support jobs as medical secretaries and orderlies.

Another big field in the category of allied health workers that has been omitted is that of medical technologist. While work performed by medical technologists provides information of great use to physicians and paramedical workers in treating a patient, they do not necessarily work alongside the physician, and their work does not parallel that of the physician to any great extent. But they are nevertheless expert in the use of highly specialized equipment such as x-ray machines, ultrasound machines, CT scanners and MRIs, and in performing electrocardiograms (EKGs). They also work in clinical laboratories performing a wide variety of tests and assays of tissue, blood, and other body fluids, which physicians rely on to help in the diagnosis and treatment of patients. The market for clinical technologists, like that of paramedicals, has grown sharply in recent years.

In this book we focus primarily on those jobs in which the workers handle functions and duties traditionally considered to be those of the physician or other health professional. Within this category of paramedicals, we will discuss the specific job requirements and responsibilities for each career and describe the training and education required to enter the field, the certification required, if any, and the salaries and opportunities for employment.

Also, because the paramedical field is so new, job titles, duties, and the nature and content of educational programs and lists of accredited schools may be in flux. In other words, these programs are more subject to change than those in a more traditional field.

While we have attempted to show salary ranges for each field, in a few cases, information was limited or nonexistent, and we had to rely on more localized information.

In all cases, we have listed the names and addresses of the appropriate professional organization to contact for information about the specific paramedical field involved.

CHAPTER 2

A QUICKLY GROWING FIELD

Just twenty-five to thirty years ago, most of the careers discussed in this book did not even exist, with the possible exception of physician assistant, which dates back to the mid-sixties. But in just a few decades, many of these paramedical careers have grown far more quickly than almost anyone could have foreseen. How could they have attained such prominence so quickly? The answer lies in a complex of factors, including the shortage of physicians, most notably primary care physicians, with whom the patient comes in contact first; the growing demand for healthcare, which can be attributed to several factors that are discussed below; and the resultant escalation of healthcare costs.

SHORTAGE OF PHYSICIANS—REAL OR IMAGINED?

In this chapter we will examine the paramedical worker as the solution to many of the healthcare manpower shortages we face. But first let's examine the matter of the physician shortage. Is there or is there not a shortage of physicians today? The answer depends on your perspective. For instance, just about everyone agrees that there is a shortage of primary care physicians, who are the ones that you most often come into contact first—internists, general practitioners, pediatricians, and obstetrician-gynecologists. Most experts agree that there is no shortage but, in fact, perhaps an over-abundance of certain physician specialists—urologists, surgeons, radiologists, and cardiologists, among others. Others say there is no shortage in any category of physicians; that it is primarily a matter of unequal distribution of physicians. In other words, most doctors, especially those specializing, are more likely to practice in larger urban areas, and as a result there is a critical shortage of physicians in rural and inner city areas. Within the limitations of this book, we cannot go into the reasons for this supposed shortage of physicians. But it is a fact that large sections of our population not only are underserved by physicians but are almost completely lacking these services, even the most basic of care.

It is further known that there has been a sharp increase in the number of physicians serving the population. In 1965 there was 1 doctor for every 697 people in the United States; by 1985 that number had dropped to 1 doctor for every 471, and today it is probably closer to 1 physician for every 400 Americans. The accounting firm of Peat Marwick estimates that at this rate, within the next few years there will be a surplus of physicians.

There is, however, a definite shortage of primary care doctors, as noted above. In fact, medical schools have been accepting ever greater numbers of students who indicate a desire to enter primary care. And since primary care doctors are the ones most likely to employ paramedicals, the demand for paramedical workers is expected to increase sharply. In fact, the Bureau of Labor Statistics has labeled many paramedical fields—including dental hygienists, physical and occupational therapy assistants, and medical assistants—among the fastest growing occupations and those with the greatest increase in employment projected by the year 2006. But, as you can see, as we discuss the various paramedical careers, the job outlook is good for all categories of paramedicals. And the demand for primary care doctors and paramedicals in the inner city and rural areas is especially keen.

THE EMERGENCE OF HMOS AND MANAGED CARE

Accounting to a great extent for this shortage of healthcare professionals, both doctors and paramedicals, is the rapid emergence of HMOs (health maintenance organizations) and managed care (referred to by some as "cookbook" medicine) with its emphasis on health maintenance and disease prevention. Add to this mix the rapid growth of nursing homes, birthing centers, community centers, emergency and surgicenters, and various other centers—some privately funded and some public agencies—and you have yet another cause for the rise in demand for healthcare specialists. Because these organizations are primarily larger and more institutional in their outlook, we can expect to see a greater demand for paramedicals to handle the more routine assignments that a doctor would in the past have performed in private practice.

There are several other factors that have sparked the demand for healthcare services, besides the shortage of physicians. For one, there is the tremendous growth in population. Today, thanks to medical science and technology, people are living longer and are better able to endure the onslaught of diseases that just a few decades ago would have wiped out thousands upon thousands of our citizens. Included in this category of killer diseases are tuberculosis, polio, pneumonia, diphtheria, and, more recently, hardening of the arteries, a leading cause of heart disease, cancer, and diabetes. Many of these former scourges—such as polio and diphtheria—have either been wiped out or are under control, and much progress has been made in reducing the number of deaths due to cancer and heart disease, among others. But accompanying this increase in aging has been a rise in the demand for medical services, since the elderly are more prone to potentially fatal or crippling diseases.

Further fueling the demand for healthcare is the fact that today most of us are covered by some form of health insurance, public or private. This was not true prior to World War II, when nearly 90 percent of Americans paid for healthcare services out of their own pockets. Now with increased numbers of our citizens covered by such federal programs as Medicare (for those over age fifty-five) and Medicaid (for those earning below the poverty level), as well as such programs as Blue Cross & Blue Shield, which covers 100 million Americans itself, healthcare is more than ever within the grasp of millions. While our parents or grandparents might have been reluctant to see a doctor or to enter a hospital unless they were desperately ill, such considerations are largely a thing of the past, since the government or private insurance picks up the healthcare bill.

Finally, there has been a sharp upsurge in our awareness and understanding of healthcare services because of greater exposure by the media; newspapers, radio, TV, and now, the Internet, are informing us about healthcare issues and technology. Every day we are bombarded by new discoveries to help diagnose and bring under control such diseases as cancer and, more recently, AIDS. As these new technologies in the diagnosis and treatment of disease are announced, we are demanding these services.

Accompanying this upsurge in demand for medical treatment and care has been a sharp increase in new drugs, healthcare services, and products. In 1993 Americans spent more than $884 billion on healthcare, roughly 11 percent of the gross national product. Healthcare is by far the fastest growing part of the GNP, far outstripping food, transportation, and shelter. In fact, economists are predicting that if present trends continue, there should be a tripling in healthcare costs within the next few years, accounting for nearly 16 percent of the GNP.

PARAMEDICALS TO THE FORE

These skyrocketing costs in healthcare have caused many in the field, especially the government, which pays an estimated 43 percent of the healthcare dollar, to seek out ways to limit these costs. And one solution that has been offered as a good alternative in medical care and treatment is the increased use of paramedical personnel. The reasoning is that with medical costs rising out of sight and large areas of the population almost devoid of medical care and services, it would make sense to train paramedicals to handle the more routine cases that present themselves to the doctor, thus freeing up the doctor to handle the more serious and complex cases that require his or her expertise.

Thus the physician would take care of the more seriously ill patients while the paramedical—in this case the physician assistant or one of the various categories of advanced practice nurses—would handle the less complex and the more routine cases. That is how the first and certainly one of the most rapidly expanding paramedical careers, the physician assistant, came into being.

In the fall of 1965, conditions were right to begin a new program to train physician assistants at Duke University. The shortage of physicians was acute, and hospital and medical corpsmen who had received excellent healthcare training in the Korean and Vietnamese wars, were seeking out new ways to utilize their training and know-how. Obviously, such corpsmen had a lot to offer and were excellent candidates to serve as clinical assistants to physicians in private practice.

From the original four corpsmen enrolled in that first class at Duke, the physician assistant program has grown, and today it encompasses several thousand students in training in more than sixty-four programs, primarily anchored at large medical centers and universities.

With this initial impetus, the program has gone on to become increasingly successful. With the support of physician assistants, doctors have been able to see roughly 40 percent more patients. By assigning such routine and relatively simple procedures as taking case histories and conducting physician exams, the doctor has been able to reserve his or her knowledge for patients requiring more specialized care. And, in the inner city and in wide stretches of rural areas, where doctors are not so available, physician assistants have stepped into the void, thus delivering a quality of healthcare to those who otherwise would be underserved or completely lacking such healthcare.

Because physician assistants can be trained at a fraction of the cost and time that it takes to train a physician, their salaries are much lower than those of the physician. This, in turn, has served as a limit on runaway healthcare costs. To put it another way, without the use of paramedicals, in this case the physician assistant or the nurse practitioner, the cost of healthcare would be much higher.

What is true of the medical profession and the physician assistant is also true of the other paramedical workers described in this book. By freeing up the more heavily trained professionals they work for—the doctor, dentist, podiatrist, or occupational or physical therapist—to concentrate on the more serious and complex cases, paramedical workers have enabled the various medical professionals to handle a much greater patient load than would otherwise be possible.

A WORD OF CAUTION

As you can see from the above discussion, the paramedical field is one that is rapidly expanding and that offers a growth potential matched by very few other fields. Even so, a few words of caution are necessary. This may not be the right field for you. As a para-medical, you will be taking orders and following the instructions of the professionals under whom you work. And you will be expected to follow these orders exactly or have a very good reason for deviating from them. If you have trouble taking orders from someone else, then you definitely should not make the consider-able investment of time and money that is required to become a paramedical.

Also, while there are many examples of paramedicals who have gone on, with additional training and experience, to reach the level of those for whom they work, you should not regard a paramedical career as a stepping-stone to another professional career. For example, if you are working as a physician assistant and aspire to become a physician, you may find your credentials as a physician assistant largely worthless, and you may have to start from scratch in studying for that profession.

The best reason to enter the paramedical field is because you believe it is right for you and not because it may serve as a stepping-stone to a higher paying and more prestigious job as a physician, dentist, etc. Although paramedicals can and do some-times advance into other professional ranks, it is more the excep-tion than the rule.

You also should understand that since many paramedical careers are so new, there is considerable flexibility in the duties you may be asked to assume. Here there are many factors that come into play: your own experience, what your supervisor thinks you should and can handle, where you work (in the inner city, for instance, or at a large metropolitan health center), and the number of patients to be seen as well as your own talents, likes, and abilities.

Worth mentioning, however, is the fact that if you don't like your present situation, you can always look for the same kind of opportunity almost anywhere else in the country.

Finally, don't expect to work a cozy nine-to-five daily schedule, five days a week. If you need this kind of regularity, then perhaps you should look for another profession. Although you may not have to put in the number of hours that your supervisor does, more often than not your hours are at least comparable to your supervisor's—and that can include evening and/or weekend shifts. This is especially true of physician assistants and nurse practitioners as well as emergency health technicians (paramedics) because patients become sick or have emergencies any hour of the day or night, seven days a week, weekends and holidays.

CHAPTER 3

TWO PHYSICIAN EXTENDERS: THE PHYSICIAN ASSISTANT AND THE ADVANCED PRACTICE NURSE

To start our review of paramedical careers, let's examine the work of two groups of paramedicals—physician assistants and advanced practice nurses. Both groups act as what is known as physician extenders—that is, they enable physicians to see more patients than would otherwise be possible. How? By handling the more routine cases that present themselves to the physician, thus freeing up the physician to concentrate his or her energies on the more serious and complex cases.

In so doing, we will have to look at some special areas or sub-groups of both careers: the surgical physician assistant, a special category of physician assistants; and the nurse practitioner, nurse anesthetist, nurse-midwife, and clinical nurse specialist, four special categories of advanced practice nurses. All advanced practice nurses, incidentally, require training over and above that required for RNs.

WHAT PHYSICIAN EXTENDERS DO

The duties of physician assistants and nurse practitioners are very similar. They conduct physical exams, take case histories, and diagnose and treat minor illnesses or injuries. They also order lab tests and x-ray exams and interpret the results; they counsel and educate patients on good health practices. In many cases, both groups accompany physicians on patient rounds in both acute, short-term hospitals and in nursing homes. Other duties in which both categories of medical workers are involved include:

- developing and putting into effect the patient management or treatment plan, recording progress notes and assisting in providing care in the office and other outpatient facilities
- handling such relatively simple procedures as injections, immunizations, suturing, and wound care
- performing and noting any deviations from normal laboratory, radiological, cardiographic, and other tests to help in patient diagnosis
- treating simple conditions produced by infection or injury and assisting in treatment of more serious illnesses, which can include helping the surgeon in performing operations and initiating diagnostic tests in response to life-threatening situations
- referring patients to appropriate community health agencies and/or medical specialists as called for
- educating and counseling patients in observing prescribed treatment plans dealing with such matters as normal growth and development, problems of everyday living, family planning, and disease prevention

Although this list is not by any means exhaustive, it does include most of the major duties of both the PA and the nurse practitioner.

Let's take a closer look at the physician assistant, who works directly under the physician in caring for patients.

THE PHYSICIAN ASSISTANT

As noted in Chapter 2, the physician assistant (PA) came into being primarily to help solve the acute shortage of medical manpower, particularly the primary care physician, which followed World War II, especially in the 1950s and 1960s. And unlike the medical specialist, who usually focuses on one particular disease or area of the body—such as the cardiologist who concentrates on heart disease, or the urologist who specializes in diseases of the urinary tract—the primary care physician treats the whole person, and quite often, all of the members of the family. Primary care physicians are called on to care for and treat patients with a wide range of illnesses and chronic medical conditions such as diabetes or arthritis, injuries, accidents, emotional problems—in short, anything that could impair the patient's health and functioning. Under these conditions, it is clear that the physician assistant can be of great help in providing medical care and thus helping to relieve the overburdened primary care physician.

This was the thinking that led to the establishment of training programs for physician assistants at Duke University, the University of Colorado, Wake Forest University, and the University of Washington in the mid-sixties. In the years intervening, PA services have expanded to the point where today PAs are working in almost all areas of medicine—specialty care as well as primary care—although primary care is still the PA's principal area of practice. It is estimated that more than half of all PAs serve in the area of primary care.

It also should be noted that no paramedical worker has been more closely studied or observed than the PA, and for good reason. In the past, only doctors were licensed to treat and diagnose patients' medical problems—until the PA. Thus the PA represents a radical departure from this practice, in that he or she is trained to specifically diagnose and treat an estimated 80 percent of the illnesses that are presented to the primary care physician.

Despite some initial concerns by the medical establishment that PAs might take over a part of their practices, today this health worker enjoys wide acceptance by both physicians and patients alike as an important member of the healthcare team.

In 1998, physician assistants, estimated at more than thirty-one thousand, nearly all graduates of PA programs, were employed all over the country. Approximately three thousand PAs enter the workforce annually, a trend that has accelerated rapidly over the years and that is expected to continue.

Physician Assistant Training Programs

PA programs, covering both the traditional and innovative in medical education, are usually two years in length leading to a bachelor's degree. Programs are offered in colleges and universities, teaching hospitals, and the military with a prerequisite involving two years of college (undergraduate) work and prior healthcare experience. A few programs run three to four years with prerequisites built into the curriculum.

Subject content in the PA program includes both classroom instruction, lab sessions, and clinical rotations (usually in the second year). In the first year, you concentrate on classes and lab work in the basic sciences and preclinical subjects. Courses most often taught include anatomy, physiology, microbiology, pharmacology, pathophysiology, physical diagnosis, and behavior science.

Following the first nine to fifteen months of training, you participate in clinical clerkships and preceptorships (a kind of apprenticeship program in which you learn from the supervising physician) in various settings such as teaching and community hospitals, clinics, long-term nursing homes, and doctors' offices. Clinical rotations most frequently are offered in obstetrics/gynecology, internal medicine, pediatrics, surgery, family medicine, psychiatry, emergency medicine, and geriatrics. It is an intensive program often involving six days of class and lab work, plus additional hours of study at home or at the library, and little if any time off for holidays or vacations.

Gaining admission to PA schools is no snap either. Many programs receive several applications for each spot. It is therefore to your interest to apply to several schools in which you may be interested to better your chances of being accepted.

Admission requirements vary, but studies show that more than half of all applicants have their college degrees. As noted above, college degrees are not required in most programs, but they do help in gaining admission. Many programs require that you have completed courses in biology, English, humanities/social sciences, chemistry, college math, and psychology.

Since school costs vary, it is recommended that you write directly to any schools in which you are interested for information on costs, scholarships, and other financial aids available, as well as information on prerequisites and the admission procedure. Almost always financial assistance in the form of federal, state, and private loans, as well as scholarships and private grants, are available.

Training programs for physician assistants are listed in Appendix A.

National Certification

To ensure that you can meet minimum standards of practice and proficiency for PAs, you are required to pass a national examination for certification given annually all over the country. Currently all states require that you be certified by the National Commission on Certification of Physician Assistants, and such certification is a prerequisite to being licensed. To be certified you must be a graduate of an accredited PA program and pass a certifying examination.

THE ADVANCED PRACTICE NURSE

Further enabling the doctor to see more patients and to deliver vital medical care services where they are needed is the advanced practice nurse. This is a broad category of nurses who have completed advanced clinical nurses' educational requirements beyond those required for all RNs. Included in this broad category of advanced practice nurses are: nurse practitioners, nurse anesthetists, nurse-midwives, and clinical nurse specialists. Of these, the one most closely allied to the PA is the nurse practitioner. It is this advanced practice nurse that we will concentrate on below, followed with a look at the other categories of advanced practice nurses.

The Nurse Practitioner

To all appearances the work of the nurse practitioner is almost identical to that of the PA. The difference lies primarily in the fact that physician assistants work directly under the supervision of and report to supervising physicians. They are taught to think and act like physicians. Nurse practitioners, on the other hand, are educated to expand the delivery of healthcare through use of nursing theory and techniques. Also, like the PA, the nurse practitioner usually works under the supervision of a physician. But in some states, nurse practitioners practice independently, seeing and treating patients on their own, without having to report to any physician supervisor.

To qualify as a nurse practitioner, you must be a registered nurse with one and a half to two years of training over and above the two- or four-year degree in nursing. In 1996, there were forty-eight thousand nurse practitioners working in various settings—hospitals, nursing homes, clinics, and in private practice. While most nurse practitioners work under the supervision of a physician, this varies from state to state, and in some states nurse practitioners have their own practices. In forty-nine states they can prescribe medication. They work both in general practice and in a wide number of specialty areas, such as pediatrics and obstetrics.

At least thirty-six states require NPs to be certified nationally by the American Nurses Association or by various nursing specialty associations, as applicable.

Nurse Practitioner Training Programs

As is true of the PA training programs, training for nurse practitioners is offered at various nursing schools. Programs usually alternate between classroom work and clinical exposure, but in the NP program there is less emphasis on the basic sciences in the first year and more on health promotion and good nutrition. Like the PA, nurse practitioners often serve a clinical internship under the supervision of a physician.

SPECIALIZED PHYSICIAN ASSISTANTS AND ADVANCED PRACTICE NURSES

Most PAs and advanced practice nurses work primarily in the area of general or family practice medicine. But recently, increased numbers of PAs and advanced practice nurses in particular are working in medical specialty areas.

In the case of PAs, there are specific programs for those who want to specialize as a surgical physician assistant at Cuyahoga Community College (Ohio), the University of Alabama, and Cornell University. For the most part, however, as a PA, you would specialize by learning on the job working for a physician specialist or by taking courses expanding your knowledge of any given specialty.

There are specialty training programs for advanced practice nurses who wish to specialize either as a nurse-midwife or nurse anesthetist. Information about these programs can be obtained from the professional organizations listed for either group at the end of this chapter.

Surgical Physician Assistant

Currently there are more than one hundred programs for PAs, of which three offer training for those interested in specializing as surgical physician assistants. As is true of all PAs, the surgical physician assistant provides patient services under the direction of the surgeon he or she works for. For this reason, the services you provide as a surgical physician assistant closely match those provided by the physician assistant—obtaining the patient's history and physical data to help the surgeon determine the diagnosis and treatment appropriate for that patient's condition. Beyond this you might assist in various procedures and tests required for the diagnosis and treatment of patients, help prepare patients for surgery, assist during the actual procedures, and help care for and counsel patients in the postoperative program.

Training programs, which average about two years in length, closely resemble those of the PA for the first year. The emphasis is on the basic sciences: microbiology, pharmacology, anatomy, and physiology. Second-year skills, however, both clinical and lecture, emphasize development of surgical skills, pre- and postoperative evaluation, and management of the patient treatment plan. Programs for surgical physical assistants are included in Appendix A under the schools noted above.

Nurse Anesthetist

Nurse anesthetists, one of the four categories of advanced practice nurses, currently number about twenty-seven thousand and are trained in administering anesthesia. They are generally credited with being the first profession to provide anesthesia services in the United States. They therefore comprise the oldest recognized body of advanced practice nurses.

As a nurse anesthetist, you work with the anesthesiologist (a medical specialist) and are responsible for selecting the proper dosage to be given during surgery and for monitoring the patient's vital signs during surgery, noting any significant changes in the patient's condition. Today, it is estimated that more than 65 percent of all anesthesia is administered by nurse anesthetists, under the supervision of the anesthesiologist.

The training program for nurse anesthetists, offered in approximately eighty-five accredited nurse anesthesia programs, lasts from twenty-four to twenty-eight months. To qualify for training as a nurse anesthetist, you must be, first of all, a graduate of an accredited school of nursing. Nearly 75 percent of all nurse anesthetists work in hospitals; the rest are in group practice or contract their services as required.

All states require nurse anesthetists to be licensed. But first you must pass a certification examination administered by the American Association of Nurse Anesthetists. Successful completion of this exam entitles you to use the designation CRNA (Certified Registered Nurse Anesthetist). To maintain certification, you must complete compulsory continuing education courses every two years.

The anesthetist's assistant (AA), not to be confused with the nurse anesthetist, performs many of the same duties as the nurse anesthetist but generally works more directly under the supervision of the anesthesiologist. Not a nurse, the AA has a bachelor's degree with a major in physical science and must complete a two-year training program, the same as the physician assistant.

Nurse-Midwife

Certified nurse-midwives, still another category of advanced practice nurses, are registered nurses trained to diagnose health problems of women and to deliver babies. In existence since colonial times, they were not formally organized until the early 1920s.

Nurse-midwives, whose skills are certified by the American College of Nurse-Midwives, provide care and support for mothers during pregnancy and supervise their progress as they approach delivery. After delivery, the nurse-midwife evaluates the health of the newborn and provides care. Often, as a midwife you are called on to assist the mother with breast- or bottle-feeding and self-care and instruct her in child development. Nurse-midwives work in a variety of settings including hospitals, clinics, health maintenance organizations (HMOs), family planning agencies, public health centers, and private physicians' offices.

Certified nurse-midwives must complete one of thirty-five training programs offered in the United States. These range from twenty-three programs awarding the master's degree to ten certificate programs and two precertification programs. In addition, as a nurse-midwife you must complete a national certification exam to be licensed to provide primary care to women in the area of obstetrics and gynecology in all fifty states. Passing the certification exam entitles you to use the initials CNM (Certified Nurse-Midwife) after your name.

Clinical Nurse Specialist

Until recently the clinical nurse specialist (CNS), the final category of advanced practice nurse, served primarily as a consultant or resource person for staff education. The nurse practitioner, on the other hand, received more training in patient care. Today, more often than not these distinctions are blurred and the possibility of merging the two groups and having most graduate nursing programs in these two areas simply offering advanced nursing degrees has been discussed.

SALARIES

What you earn as a PA or as an advanced practice nurse depends on several factors: the kind of practice you work for (if you work for a surgeon, for example, you will make more than if you work for a family practitioner), geographical location, experience, and your educational background.

In 1997, the average median national income for PAs was just over $61,000 per year. If you worked in a hospital or medical office, you earned slightly more than if you worked in a clinic. With five years or more of experience, your salary would average from $50,000 to $55,000 a year, and you might earn as much as $100,000 a year. If you worked for the federal government, your salary would average $39,600 per year.

Nurse anesthetists averaged $86,000 according to a recent survey of the American Association of Nurse Anesthetists. This figure included both salary income and overtime. Nurse anesthetists who run their own businesses can expect to earn considerably more, although they should expect lower earnings for the first few years of operation while they are becoming established.

A 1996 survey by the Hay Group of HMOs, group practices, and hospital-based clinics showed that nurse practitioners' salaries averaged $66,800 and ranged from $54,000 to $69,000. The same survey showed nurse-midwives earning about $70,100 per year, with ranges from $59,300 to $75,700 per year.

THE FUTURE

Although there has been some lessening of demand for both PAs and advanced practice nurses, the employment outlook is nevertheless excellent for the immediate future. In recent years, the demand for healthcare services has shifted from inpatient surgery to outpatient surgery, and hospital stays have been considerably shortened. Also, because of the downsizing of many corporation staffs, many individuals are foregoing or postponing hospital treatment or surgery for as long as possible.

Nevertheless, the federal government has foreseen increasing shortages in both PAs and advanced practice nurses for the next twenty years. The U.S. Department of Labor lists the PA career among its top fifteen career choices and anticipates a 46.6 percent increase in the number of PA jobs by the year 2006. With the right credentials and certification, both PAs and advanced practice nurses should have no trouble finding positions in a wide range of healthcare facilities.

Even though these two professions have had good acceptance by both physicians and patients, there are still some doctors who refuse to hire either nurse practitioners or PAs. It should be noted that the number of physicians per 100,000 Americans keeps on rising and presumably could cause a reduction in the demand for both PAs and nurse practitioners. But since graduates in both groups can be hired at a fraction of the cost of recent M.D. graduates, it seems safe to conclude that the numbers of PAs and nurse practitioners will continue to rise in the near future. Then, too, the government continues to relax restrictions on the use of PAs and nurse practitioners. For example, Medicare now allows physicians to bill the government for services provided by PAs in all settings.

Benefits for both PAs and advanced practice nurses are good. If you are employed in private clinics or government facilities or in hospitals or short-term facilities, you will most likely enjoy such attractive benefits as paid vacations, holidays, and sick days as well as participation in pension and investment programs. You also will qualify for healthcare coverage not only for yourself but for your family as well.

LEGAL CONSIDERATIONS

These days, with the incidence of malpractice suits a very real consideration in the practice of medicine, should you as a PA or advanced practice nurse be concerned? The answer is a qualified yes, since both the physician and the PA or advanced practice nurse who works in his or her office share in their liability in such malpractice suits. However, since this is the case, it is highly unlikely that your physician employer would authorize you to do work beyond your capability and experience.

It should be further noted that studies have shown that when PAs are employed, patients on the whole are highly pleased because waiting periods are reduced, they receive more attention, and doctor-patient relationships are improved, which tends to reduce the risk of malpractice suits.

FOR MORE INFORMATION

American Academy of Nurse Practitioners
  LBJ Building
  P.O. Box 12845, Capitol Station
  Austin, TX 78711

American Academy of Physician Assistants
  950 N. Washington Street
  Alexandria, VA 22314-1552

American Association of Nurse Anesthetists
  222 S. Prospect Street
  Park Ridge, IL 60068-4001

American College of Nurse-Midwives
  1522 K Street, NW, Suite 1000
  Washington, DC 20005

American Nurses Association
  600 Maryland Avenue, SW, Suite 100W
  Washington, DC 20024-2571

Association of Physician Assistant Programs
  950 N. Washington Street
  Alexandria, VA 22314-1552

Commission on Accreditation of Allied Health Programs
  35 E. Wacker Drive, Suite 1970
  Chicago, IL 60601

National League for Nursing
  350 Hudson Street
  New York, NY 10014

CHAPTER 4

OTHER PARAMEDICAL WORKERS IN MEDICINE

While most physician assistants, except for surgeon assistants, do not require certification in any particular area of medicine, there are a few areas in paramedical careers where this does not hold true. In this chapter, we discuss those paramedical careers that do require specialty certification—podiatric assistant and pathologist assistant.

THE PODIATRIC ASSISTANT

Podiatry is that area of medicine concentrating on the diagnosis, treatment, and prevention of diseases of the human foot. To become a podiatrist, you must successfully complete a four-year training program leading to a D.P.M. (Doctor of Podiatric Medicine). In addition, you must pass a state licensing exam to practice in any state.

What Is a Podiatric Assistant?

As a podiatric assistant, as is the case of all paramedicals, you are qualified by your schooling and clinical experience to serve patients under the direction of a licensed podiatrist.

Like other health paramedicals, what you do as a podiatric assistant will depend largely on your experience and training, the kind of podiatric practice in which you work, and the volume of patients seen, as well as the number of additional assistants employed. What follows is a list of common duties you might perform:

- preparing patients for treatment, including padding and strapping
- taking and recording patient histories
- applying surgical dressings
- preparing and sterilizing instruments and equipment
- providing postoperative instructions to the patient
- exposing and developing x-rays
- assisting in biomedical evaluation and negative castings
- handling routine office procedures, including answering the telephone, scheduling appointments, and maintaining inventory

Education and Certification

It's true that most podiatric assistants receive their training on the job, but you may be eligible to be awarded the designation PMAC (Podiatric Medical Assistant—Certified) from the American Society of Podiatric Medicine. To qualify, you must be a member of the society and pass a written exam given by the society. In addition, you must complete a number of continuing education courses every year to retain certification.

Job Outlook

Job prospects for podiatric assistants should remain good for many years. Most podiatrists currently employ at least two assistants, and that number is expected to rise. As our population ages, the demand for treatment of foot problems should rise, and podiatrists will rely increasingly on podiatric assistants to handle routine measurements.

For More Information

American Society of Podiatric Medical Assistants
  2124 S. Austin Boulevard
  Cicero, IL 60804

THE PATHOLOGIST ASSISTANT

A pathologist is a medical doctor who specializes in the study, analysis, and diagnosis of changes caused by diseases of the tissue and the blood. To qualify, he or she must have completed medical training and have taken specialized residency training in pathology. To qualify as a pathologist assistant, you would need educational background and experience to assist the pathologist in the preparation, dissection, and completion of work with autopsy and specimens obtained through surgery.

Job Functions

Depending on the pathologist for whom you work, these are a few of the tasks that you might be required to perform as a pathologist assistant:

- assist in autopsies, including external examination, on-site organ inspections, evisceration or removal of internal organs, and dissection of organs and tissue
- obtaining biological specimens for analysis (blood cultures, viral cultures, toxicological material, and so on)
- dictation of or recording of data on your findings

- assisting the pathologist in preparation of preliminary diagnoses and summarizing the clinical history of same
- gross description and complete dissection of surgical specimens
- selecting and submitting tissue sections for microscopic analysis (that is, frozen and permanent sections for light, electron, and fluorescent microscopy) for both postmortem examinations and for examination of human surgical specimens

Working with diseased tissue of the dead does require a certain amount of dedication and fortitude. If you think you would be uncomfortable in dissecting corpses or handling diseased tissue, you might do well to consider some other paramedical career.

Education and Training

While some pathologist assistants receive their training on the job, there are five schools that offer training programs in this area. Programs vary in length and in the degree awarded. Usually the pathologist assistant program runs two years in length—one year of academic work and a year of clinical training.

Certification

At present there is no national certification or licensing examination for pathologist assistants. The American Association of Pathologists Assistants (AAPA) does administer a competency exam to its 350 members, but this is completely voluntary. You need not pass this exam to work in this area. A few states, however, require that you be licensed as a pathologist assistant to work in that state.

Salaries

Salaries for pathologist assistants currently range between $45,000 and $75,000 a year. As a beginner, in some parts of the country, you might earn a salary as high as $55,000 a year; with experience and a master's degree, you might receive a salary of $75,000 a year.

For More Information

For information on careers as a pathologist assistant, write to:

American Association of Pathologist Assistants
  1711 West County Road B, Suite 300N
  Roseville, MN 55113

CHAPTER 5

THE MEDICAL ASSISTANT

It would be quite simple to take the terms *medical assistant* and *physician assistant* to mean the same thing, but don't get the two confused. There is a world of difference between them. To be sure, they both offer substantial support to the physician, but they are not the same. PAs serve as physician extenders, as noted in Chapter 3. They enable the physician to serve more patients than would otherwise be possible. They see, examine, and treat patients under the direction of a physician and are, in effect, practicing medicine, but they do not do so independently.

Medical assistants, on the other hand, while they provide invaluable support to physicians through their skills and services, also serve as clerks or administrators and secretaries in doctors' offices. In effect, they are the intermediary between doctors and their patients and help to keep their offices running smoothly. That explains in great part why nearly all physicians in practice today have at least one skilled medical assistant in their office. To put it simply, the medical assistant is the link between the doctor and the patient and between the doctor and professional colleagues and/or suppliers of medications and equipment.

With more than 225,000 persons presently employed as medical assistants, this is by far the largest of the paramedical careers. Two organizations accredit medical assisting programs: The Commission on Accreditation of Allied Health Education Programs

(CAAHEP) and the Accrediting Bureau of Health Education Schools (ABHES). As of 1998, more than sixty thousand medical assistants have been certified by the American Association of Medical Assistants and designated as Certified Medical Assistants. An additional sixty thousand carry the registered designation of the American Medical Technologists, the other professional organization for medical assistants.

WHAT MEDICAL ASSISTANTS DO

By taking the burden of running the office off of the shoulders of physicians so that they can concentrate on diagnosing and treating patients, medical assistants' services are invaluable to the physician. Specific duties vary from office to office, depending on the size and location of the office and the physician's specialty. But the backbone of your job as a medical assistant may include any of the following clinical or patient-oriented duties that you have been trained to handle:

- taking medical histories
- preparing patients for examination and assisting as the doctor examines them
- recording vital signs—pulse, blood pressure, temperature, etc.
- sterilizing medical equipment and instruments
- disposing of contaminated supplies
- collecting and preparing laboratory specimens and performing basic laboratory tests on blood and urine in the physician's office
- preparing and administering medications as directed by the doctor
- instructing patients on medication usage and diet
- authorizing drug refills as directed by the doctor

- handling such procedures as drawing blood, taking EKGs, removing stitches, changing dressings, and preparing patients for x-rays

In addition to these duties you may be responsible for arranging examining rooms and equipment, purchasing and maintaining supplies, keeping the premises clean, and so forth. Specific duties are prescribed by state law.

Other duties you may be required to handle are basically clerical:

- answering phone calls and receiving patients
- scheduling appointments, updating and filling out insurance forms and records, and arranging for hospital admissions, lab services, or other medical treatments
- handling billing and bookkeeping

EDUCATIONAL PROGRAMS

The days when you might have received training as a medical assistant right on the job are long gone. Today, because the operation and handling of medical care have become so complex and the job requirements so demanding, few doctors have the time or can provide on-the-job training for their staff.

Instead, most likely you would receive your training at one of several hundred programs located all over the country that are accredited by one of the two accrediting agencies—the previously mentioned Commission on Accreditation of Allied Health Education Programs, which accredits approximately four hundred programs, and the Accrediting Bureau of Health Education Schools, which accredits an additional two hundred programs. For a list of programs accredited by the CAAHEP, see Appendix B. For programs accredited by the ABHES, contact them directly at the address shown at the end of the chapter.

If you plan to become a medical assistant and are still in high school, courses that will prove especially helpful include: basic secretarial classes, typing, mathematics, English, and courses in the health sciences.

As a student in an accredited medical assistant program, courses you are likely to study include: anatomy, physiology, medical terminology, medical law and ethics, psychology, oral and written communication, bookkeeping, insurance, and administrative and clerical procedures. An externship in a physician's office is required to provide practical experience.

CERTIFICATION

You can obtain certification, which is highly desirable in landing a job and advancing in this career, if you are a graduate of an accredited program. If so, you can apply for the examinations offered by either the American Association of Medical Assistants (AAMA) or the American Medical Technologists (AMT). The AAMA awards the Certified Medical Assistant designation, while the AMT awards the Registered Medical Assistant certification. The AAMA certification exam is given annually in January and June at more than two hundred test centers throughout the United States. The AMT exam is given throughout the year at various testing centers in the United States.

Certification indicates your performance is up to certain standards, which physicians increasingly are looking for in hiring their medical assistants.

EARNINGS

Your salary as a medical assistant, as is true of virtually all paramedical careers, will depend on local salary scales, your background and experience, and where you work, as well as specific job responsibilities. For instance, a recent AAMA survey showed that primarily administrative medical assistants earn more than those whose duties are primarily clinical. As you would expect, average salary increases with experience. Thus as a medical assistant with two years or fewer of experience, you would earn $16,725 a year, while your salary would jump to an average of $24,711 a year with eleven or more years of experience.

Medical assistants whose duties were primarily administrative averaged $21,244 a year, while those with more than half clinical assignments averaged $20,775. Similarly, your work setting can affect your earnings. For instance, if you worked for a doctor in solo practice, you would average $21,888, whereas if you worked for a group practice, you would average $20,916 a year, and if your employer was connected with an HMO or managed care facility, you would average $18,965.

Location also affects salaries, with the highest earnings reported in New England, the middle Atlantic, and Pacific states, and the lowest in the east and west north central states and the east and west south central states.

JOB OUTLOOK

The Bureau of Labor Statistics has projected the medical assistant as one of the fastest growing occupations in terms of numbers employed from 1996 to 2006. For that period, the BLS shows a nearly 80 percent increase in the number of medical assistants working, or an increase of better than 200,000 workers. This is due to several factors: the expansion in healthcare jobs due to the increased medical needs of an aging population, increases in the number of physicians, more diagnostic and test procedures, and finally, more paperwork. Most job openings, however, will result from the need to replace those who have left the profession, died, or retired.

FOR MORE INFORMATION

Additional information about medical assisting can be obtained from:

Accrediting Bureau of Health Education Schools
    803 W. Broad Street, Suite 730
    Falls Church, VA 22046

American Association of Medical Assistants
    20 N. Wacker Drive, Suite 1575
    Chicago, IL 60606-2903

American Medical Technologists
    70 Higgins Road
    Park Ridge, IL 60068-5765

CHAPTER 6

EMERGENCY MEDICAL TECHNICIANS

Every day in communities large and small across the United States, frantic calls come in on the emergency 911 network or to hospitals or emergency centers for help to persons who have experienced life and death injuries involving automobile accidents, heart attacks, strokes, poisonings, accidental electrocution, near drownings, gunshot wounds, and many other situations requiring immediate medical attention.

Usually the first ones on the scene are the EMTs or emergency medical technicians, more commonly known as paramedics. Working under the instructions of medical officers at a central office, EMTs work in teams of two and drive specially equipped emergency vehicles (ambulances) to the scene of the emergency. They may work for the police or fire departments, for hospitals, or for private ambulance services or rescue squads. Arriving on the scene, they render first aid or cardiopulmonary resuscitation (CPR) to victims of heart attacks, strokes, near drownings, and other similar medical emergencies. If necessary, they may request additional help on the scene from police, fire, or electric company workers, or they may seek volunteer help from bystanders in directing traffic or removing obstacles.

Next, they try to find out the nature and seriousness of the patient's injuries or illness or if he or she has any preexisting conditions such as heart problems, epilepsy, or diabetes that could affect their condition. Following strict guidelines for the procedures they perform, they provide prescribed medical treatment.

WHAT EMERGENCY MEDICAL TECHNICIANS DO

There are several levels of paramedics, and what you can do will depend largely upon which category you fall into. All EMTs, including those with basic skills only, the EMT-basic classification, can handle the following procedures after having determined the extent of injuries and kinds of treatment called for:

- treating for shock, administering oxygen or CPR
- immobilizing fractures, bandaging wounds
- opening airways, restoring breathing, controlling bleeding
- rendering first-aid treatment to heart attack or accident victims, disturbed patients, or poison or burn victims
- using a defibrillator to give lifesaving shocks to patients whose heartbeat may be faint or may have stopped altogether

EMT-intermediates, the next category of EMTs, also known at EMT-Is, have more advanced training and can handle such additional procedures as using advanced airways techniques and equipment to assist patients experiencing breathing problems, as well as the use of other intensive care equipment.

The last category of EMTs, EMT-paramedics, have had the most extensive training and, in addition to the procedures listed above, are qualified to handle such procedures as:

- administering drugs by mouth or intravenously
- interpreting and reading electrocardiograms (EKGs)
- performing endotracheal intubation
- using monitors and other complex equipment

In some cases, conditions are simple enough for you to handle as an EMT on the spot; others are more complicated and can be handled only under the step-by-step direction of doctors with whom you may be in radio contact.

Since emergencies can happen at any time, day or night and on weekends, you may be called on to work odd shifts and in harsh weather. And there is always the possibility that you may have to work the midnight shift, weekends, and even holidays.

TRAINING AND OTHER QUALIFICATIONS

To qualify for even the lowest level of EMT—EMT-basic—you must have at least 100 hours of classroom work plus 10 hours of internship in a hospital emergency room. Training is offered in all fifty states and the District of Columbia by police, fire, and health departments, both in hospitals and as a nondegree program in colleges and universities.

In EMT school, you learn to use and care for common emergency equipment such as backboards, splints, suction devices, and oxygen delivery systems. You also would be instructed in handling bleeding emergencies, fractures, airway obstructions, heart attacks, and other common emergency procedures.

As an EMT-intermediate, you would receive an additional 35 to 55 hours of training in such procedures as patient evaluation (triage), handling intravenous fluids, and handling blockages of the esophageal airways.

Programs of instruction for the highest EMT category—EMT-paramedic—involve between 750 and 2,000 additional hours of instruction. Because of the strenuous training involved in this area, you would most likely be in a paid position. In all categories of EMT, refresher courses and continuing education are available.

To apply for EMT training, you must be at least eighteen with a high school diploma or equivalent and a driver's license. You should be emotionally stable, able to lift and carry heavy loads, and have good physical dexterity. In addition, you need good eyesight (eyeglass or contact lens correctable) with accurate perception. If you are employed by a police or fire department, you also must be trained as a firefighter or police officer.

For a list of accredited training programs, see Appendix C.

CERTIFICATION

To earn the registered EMT-basic designation, you must have completed an approved EMT-basic course and pass a written and practical examination given by the state regulatory agency or the National Registry of Emergency Medical Technicians. Beyond this, you must have completed the additional classwork and clinical experience and internship required to take the EMT-intermediate exam offered either by your state regulatory agency or the National Registry of Emergency Medical Technicians. To take the examination of EMT-paramedic designation, you must in addition have completed the EMT-paramedic training program and have passed a written and practical examination.

Certification requirements for the various levels of EMT vary from state to state. In some forty states you must be registered with the National Registry at some or all levels of certification. Other states require that you pass their own certifying exams at the various levels.

But to maintain your certification at any level, you must reregister, usually every two to three years, and you must be working as an EMT and be able to meet a continuing education requirement.

EARNINGS

Earnings will depend on such variables as your employer (public or private agency), locality, and your background and experience. In 1996, the Bureau of Labor Statistics reported that all EMTs in the EMT-basic category averaged $25,051, while those classified as EMT-paramedics earned $30,407 per year.

Earnings of those in the EMT-basic category working for fire departments averaged $29,859 and in the EMT-paramedic category averaged $32,483. On the other hand, EMT-basics working for hospitals averaged only $18,686, while those classified as EMT-paramedics averaged $28,383 if they were employed by hospitals. Finally, EMT-basics employed by private ambulance services averaged $18,617, and EMT-paramedics averaged $23,995. Benefits for EMTs employed by either fire or police departments are similar to those for other firefighters or police officers.

JOB OUTLOOK

Opportunities for EMTs will vary somewhat depending upon where they are employed. Competition will be especially keen in police, fire, and rescue units that pay the most and offer the best benefits. But job openings in hospitals and private ambulance services will not be so competitive since they pay less and offer less attractive benefits. Aside from that, the same forces that serve to spur the entire array of paramedical careers will be at work here: the aging and expansion of the population with accompanying need for more medical treatment. Also expected to generate more jobs is the fact that increasing numbers of communities are switching from volunteer ambulance services to paid ones. But turnover is high, reflecting the stress that you work under as an EMT, the limited chances for advancement, and the relatively modest pay scales, especially when working for private companies.

FOR MORE INFORMATION

For additional information on a career as an EMT, contact:

National Association of Emergency Medical Technicians
408 Monroe Street
Clinton, MS 39056

National Registry of Emergency Medical Technicians
P.O. Box 29233
Columbus, OH 43229

U.S. Department of Transportation
National Highway Traffic Safety Administration
Emergency Medical Services Branch
400 Seventh Avenue, SW
Washington, DC 20590

CHAPTER 7

ALLIED DENTAL PARAMEDICALS

A dentist's office is almost invariably a busy place, and the chances are that in any dentist's office, you will find between two to five people employed. The average number of allied dental paramedicals per dentist's office is 3.5. The people who work for the dentist may wear similar jackets and may look alike, but their duties vary considerably as will be seen in this chapter, which focuses on three different dental paramedicals—the dental assistant, the dental hygienist, and the dental laboratory technician.

THE DENTAL ASSISTANT

Like their equivalents in medicine, *medical assistants,* dental assistants might be described as the dentist's first assistant. Duties of dental assistants encompass both working with patients and administrative and clinical functions.

For years dental assistants, like medical assistants, were trained on the job. But because of the increasing complexities of the job and ever-increasing need to focus on professional duties, dental assistants are now almost always graduates of accredited programs and can take examinations for certification, as do medical assistants.

Dental hygienists, on the other hand, have never been trained on the job. Even in Alabama, where there is a preceptorship program (where the hygienist is trained by a supervising worker), students receive some formal classroom education.

What They Do

Both dental assistants and dental hygienists support the dentist in providing dental care to patients. But the duties performed by the dental hygienist are generally more complex and require more training than those handled by the dental assistant. Both, however, are indispensable in the handling of any modern dental practice and are members of the dental team.

Although specific duties you would perform as a dental assistant vary with the dental practice and the laws of the state in which the practice is located, generally the tasks that you would handle include, but are not restricted to, the following:

- taking and developing dental radiographs (x-rays)
- obtaining the patient's medical history and taking blood pressure and pulse
- developing infection control procedures and preparing and sterilizing instruments and equipment
- helping patients feel comfortable before, during, and after dental treatment
- providing patients with instructions following surgery or other dental treatments, such as the placement of a restoration (or filling)
- taking impressions of patients' teeth for study casts (or models of teeth)

In addition to all of these duties involving patients, you also may handle a variety of administrative duties in the office such as:

- performing office management tasks involving the use of a personal computer
- contacting patients and suppliers, scheduling appointments, answering the telephone, handling the patient billing, and ordering supplies
- assisting in all dental specialties, including orthodontics (straightening teeth with braces and corrective devices), pediatric dentistry (for children), periodontics (pertaining to tissue and structure surrounding the teeth), and oral surgery (the extraction of teeth)

Educational Programs

Nearly all of the approximately 245 dental assisting programs accredited by the American Dental Association's Commission on Dental Accreditation take nine to eleven months of full-time study to complete. A few schools offer accelerated courses, training via distance education (satellite or outlying sites of various schools), and other programs for part-time students if you are working. A few two-year programs are offered in community colleges. Here you would receive an associate degree instead of the certificate or diploma awarded in one-year programs.

The curriculum includes both classroom and lab work and preclinical instruction in dental assisting skills. You may work in dental schools, clinics, and, in some cases, dental offices, as part of your training.

All programs require at least a high school diploma or its equivalent, and a few require typing or a science course to be admitted. Useful high school courses include mathematics, chemistry, biology, and typing. In addition you might be asked to come in for a personal interview and a physical and dental examination.

A typical curriculum would include: biological sciences, including human biology, microbiology, and nutrition; dental sciences, including dental materials, oral anatomy, physiology, and oral pathology and therapeutics; dental assisting, including principles of chairside assisting and practice management; and general studies such as communications and psychology.

Certification

With two years on-the-job experience and completion of a dental assisting program, you are eligible to take the examinations given by the Dental Assisting National Board (DANB) that can result in certification. Several certificates awarded include: certified dental assistant, certified oral and maxillofacial surgery assistant, certified dental practice management assistant, and certified orthodontic assistant. Certificates are renewable annually by completing a continuing education requirement.

As an alternative to DANB certification, the American Medical Technologists (AMT) also offers certification for dental assistants. Those dental assistants certified by the AMT are designated Registered Dental Assistant, RDA (AMT). In addition, the AMT also offers the Dental Assisting Radiological Certificate, for those who have proven their competency in the radiological area of dental assisting.

Although certification is not always required to find a job, it does show that you have achieved a certain level of competence in dental assisting and can considerably improve your chances of finding initial employment. It also can help you find a job if you should move from one section of the country to another.

Some states require that you pass a certification exam for that state before you can perform specific tasks as a dental assistant. And as dental assistants assume greater patient care responsibility, more and more states will require certification.

Earnings

What you earn as a dental assistant will depend, of course, on what your employer is willing to pay, but your background and experience and the specific duties that you are responsible for will have a bearing on your salary. Geographic location, too, is another factor that can affect earnings.

In general, the pay you receive as a dental assistant is equal to that of other healthcare personnel with similar training and experience, such as medical assistants and physical therapy assistants.

In 1996, the Bureau of Labor Statistics reported that median weekly earnings for dental assistants working full-time were $361. If you were in the middle 50 percent in earnings you made between $284 and $452 a week, and the top 10 percent earned better than $516 per week.

Experienced dental assistants working thirty-two hours or more a week in private practice averaged $406 a week in 1995, according to the American Dental Association.

In addition, many dental assistants receive benefit packages including health and disability insurance, reimbursement of fees for joining professional organizations, allowances for uniforms, and paid vacations.

Job Outlook

In 1998, the American Medical Association's *Directory of Health Professions Education* reported that 84 percent of all graduates of accredited dental assisting programs found jobs within six months of graduation. So, to put it simply, the future for dental assistants looks very promising for several reasons: First, more and more workers are covered by dental insurance plans and can therefore afford dental services. Second, the public is increasingly aware of the importance of dental care. And finally, younger dentists just opening their practices as well as older dentists who are increasingly aware of the importance of competent dental assistants are spurring the demand for more dental assistants.

Your best bet for obtaining employment is in a private dental office, but jobs also can be found in hospital dental services, government services (civilian or military), dental assisting educational programs, public health dentistry, dental school clinics, and insurance companies as processors of dental claims.

For More Information

For additional information on certification or a career as a dental assistant, contact:

American Dental Assistants Association (ADAA)
666 N. Lake Shore Drive
Chicago, IL 60611

For information on the alternative certification program of the AMT, contact

American Medical Technologists
710 Higgins Road
Park Ridge, IL 60068

THE DENTAL HYGIENIST

In a manner of speaking, the dental hygienist is one step up the ladder from the dental assistant. Basically, your job as a dental hygienist is to work with the dentist in promoting sound oral hygiene and in instructing patients on how to practice good oral hygiene. There may be some overlap in what both you and the dental assistant do, but there is no doubt that what you do is higher on the scale of responsibilities and in the pay you receive.

What They Do

Perhaps the primary difference between what you do as a dental hygienist and what you would do as a dental assistant is that your tasks as the former are more directed to patient care and oral hygiene and less to administrative tasks. Depending on state regulations, your duties as a dental hygienist cover a wide range of services:

- patient screening services such as assessing oral health conditions, review of health history, oral cancer screening, head and neck inspection, dental charting, and taking blood pressure and pulse
- taking and developing dental x-rays
- removing calculus and plaque (hard and soft deposits) from all teeth surfaces
- applying preventive materials to guard against plaque (sealants and fluorides)
- teaching patients appropriate oral hygiene strategies to maintain oral health (including toothbrushing, flossing, and nutritional counseling)
- making impressions of patients' teeth for study casts (models of teeth used by dentists to evaluate patient treatment needs)
- performing documentation and office management activities

Although these are the primary duties you might handle as a dental hygienist, there are many others that dental hygienists might perform, depending on the dental practice.

Educational Requirements

As a dental hygienist, unlike the dental assistant, you must be licensed to work in all states. Besides completing an accredited program, you also must pass both written and clinical exams.

More than two hundred dental hygienist programs are currently offered.

Currently there are three kinds of programs for dental hygienists: most schools offer an associate (two-year) degree, a few offer a bachelor's degree, and six universities offer a master's degree.

The associate degree, involving two years of study, is good enough for most jobs in a private dental practice. However, a bachelor's and sometimes master's degree are required for positions involving research, teaching, or working with patients in public or school programs.

Most dental hygiene programs prefer that you have completed at least a year of college study, but some require that you have two years of college completed. You should check with the schools in which you are interested for specific admissions requirements. Admission to most dental hygiene programs is competitive, and to be accepted, you should at least have your high school diploma and a solid background in math and science.

The dental hygiene curriculum is based on a variety of courses involving classroom instruction as well as laboratory work and exposure to patients. Courses offered usually include anatomy, physiology, chemistry, microbiology, pharmacology, nutrition, pathology, dental radiology, and dental materials.

The clinical aspect of the program—in which you work with patients—includes supervised practical dental hygiene experiences plus such courses as chairside dental assisting, dental health education, community health, and so forth. In addition, you can take liberal arts courses in English, psychology, sociology, and speech.

Licensing Requirements

As noted above, to work as a dental hygienist, you must be licensed to practice in each of the fifty states. The National Board

Dental Hygiene Examination, accepted in all states, is a written exam that you must pass. You must also pass a state or regional examination testing your skills in working with patients.

Earnings

The American Dental Association reported that in 1995 dental hygienists who worked thirty-two hours or more in private practice earned about $759 a week. Earnings vary, of course, on the kind of employer you work for, geographical location, your education, and experience. If you work in a private dental office, you may be paid on an hourly, daily, salary, or commission basis or a combination of salary and commission.

Benefits vary a lot depending upon where you work and if you are working full-time or not. Dental hygienists who work for public health agencies, school systems, or the federal government usually enjoy substantial benefits.

Job Outlook

As is true of dental assistants, the outlook for dental hygienists is excellent for many of the same reasons as those applying to dental assistants: newer dentists are more apt to employ dental hygienists, and dental practices are expected to expand to meet the demands of an aging population.

Dental hygienists held 133,000 jobs in 1996, a substantial increase over the 100,000 employed in 1994. And job opportunities are expected to grow much faster than is true of other careers as a whole through 2005.

For More Information

For career information about the dental hygienist, contact:

American Dental Hygienists Association (ADHA)
444 N. Michigan Avenue, Suite 3400
Chicago, IL 60611

THE DENTAL LABORATORY TECHNICIAN

You might consider the dental laboratory technician as an artist, requiring an artist's creativity and touch as he or she constructs a variety of dental appliances—crowns, bridges, dentures, and so forth—to the dentist's specifications or prescription. Working from the dentist's orders and a mold of the patient's mouth, which contains impressions of the teeth, the dental technician first creates a plaster model of the patient's teeth, which forms the basis of the appliance to be made. It is work that is highly precise and complex, involving several stages of effort. And, in addition, you must have special skills in the use of small hand instruments and in accuracy, artistic ability, and attention to minute detail.

While most dental laboratory technicians work in dental laboratories, some work right in the dentist's office, where they are readily accessible.

Educational Requirements

Most dental laboratory technicians learn their skills right on the job, but it may take several years to become a skilled craftsperson in this field. And it could take several years more to become recognized as an accomplished worker.

Besides learning the skills on the job, there are approximately thirty-four accredited dental laboratory programs available at community and junior colleges and vocational schools as well as the military. Programs are usually two years long and include both classroom and laboratory instruction in such subjects as dental materials science, oral anatomy, fabrication procedures, and ethics.

To be accepted at most schools, you must be a high school graduate. But it should be stressed that while academic training is a plus in this field, you still may need to obtain some additional on-the-job training since laboratories differ in how they do the work.

Certification, which is optional, is offered by the National Board for Certification in Dental Laboratory Technology in five specialty areas: crown and bridge, ceramics, partial dentures, complete dentures, and orthodontic appliances.

Earnings

What you earn as a dental laboratory technician will depend primarily on your skills and the responsibilities called for in the specific position where you are employed. In general, salaries for dental technicians are equal to those of personnel in other health-care occupations.

According to the Bureau of Labor Statistics, salaries for all workers in dental laboratories averaged $23,723 in late 1995. According to limited information available, you can expect to earn only slightly more than minimum wage to begin with. However, your earnings rise sharply with experience. If you are especially productive and able to carve exact replicas from models, you might make $50,000 or more a year. In general, you can expect to earn more if you are self-employed than if you are salaried.

Job Outlook

With advancements in technology and materials, there is an increased demand for skilled dental laboratory technicians. Even so, employment of dental laboratory technicians is expected to grow more slowly than average through the year 2006, due to changes in dental care, which, in summary, have improved the overall dental health of the population. But with the aging of the population in general has come an increased interest in dental appliances for cosmetic purposes.

For More Information

For additional information on a career as a dental laboratory technician, write:

Commission on Dental Accreditation
211 E. Chicago Avenue
Chicago, IL 60611

National Association of Dental Laboratories
8201 Greenboro Drive, Suite 300
McLean, VA 22102

National Board for Certification in Dental Laboratory Technology
8201 Greensboro Drive, Suite 300
McLean, VA 22102

CHAPTER 8

EYE CARE PARAMEDICALS

Chances are that you will find paramedicals in the office of any medical professional, and this is certainly true of eye care. Visit the office of any ophthalmologist, for instance, and you most likely will find several paramedicals working alongside him or her: ophthalmic assistants, technicians, and technologists and, in a few offices, yet another paramedical, the orthoptist.

In the same manner, you will find still another eye care paramedical working in the optometrist's office—the optometric assistant and/or optometric technician. This chapter concentrates on the various categories of eye care paramedicals, and we begin with the optometric assistant.

THE OPTOMETRIC ASSISTANT AND TECHNICIAN

As is true of virtually all other categories of paramedicals, optometric assistants and technicians, also called paraoptometrics, clear the decks for the optometrist, so to speak, by taking a good deal of the routine tasks that require handling off of his or her shoulders. For example, they prepare patients for eye examinations, perform medical histories, conduct simple eye tests and record the results of same, measure patients for eye glasses that fit correctly and are comfortable, make minor adjustments on completed eyeglasses, and work with the optometrist in advising patients on how to use and maintain contact lenses. Thus they free up the optometrist for the more complex aspects of his or her practice.

Optometric assistants and technicians also handle many administrative chores: scheduling appointments, handling bookkeeping, typing and filing, keeping patient records, and maintaining inventories of supplies and materials.

Because their training is lengthier and more intensive than that of optometric assistants, optometric technicians are qualified to handle more complex tasks such as vision tests, recording eye pressures, and so on, but this does vary according to the practice for which you work.

Other Tasks Performed

Besides the duties listed above, here are several more you would typically perform as a paraoptometric:

- handling tests of color vision, acuity, and visual field
- performing facial and frame measurements and assisting patients in selecting frames
- determining the power of old and new lenses
- ordering lenses prescribed by the optometrist
- serving as chairside assistant to record data obtained during the optometrist's examination
- working with children with visual problems who require visual training

Educational Requirements

While most paraoptometrics were at one time trained in the office, as the job has become increasingly complex, few if any optometrists are willing to take the time involved in training paraoptometric personnel. Increasingly, the training function is falling to various community colleges, technical institutes, and colleges of optometry that offer one-year courses to train would-be optometric assistants. There are also some two-year programs in community colleges specifically aimed at training the higher level optometric technicians.

As is true of most paramedical training programs, courses combine classwork with technical studies. They include such courses as anatomy and physiology of the eye, vision training exercises to correct eye problems, and contact lens theory and practice. In addition, most programs offer courses in office practice.

To qualify for training as a paraoptometric, you must be a high school graduate. Courses that will prove helpful in qualifying for the work are English, math, science, and office procedures.

Certification

To be allowed to take the registration examination for paraoptometrics, you must fulfill the training and experience requirements of the American Optometric Association Paraoptometric Registry. Depending on the level of your credentials, you can be registered either as an optometric assistant or as an optometric technician. Registration is entirely voluntary, but increasingly, optometrists are looking for such certification in hiring and advancing their paraoptometric personnel. To renew your certification, you are required to complete a continuing education requirement.

Earnings

Your earnings as a paraoptometric will depend upon geographical location, kind of practice, size of practice, and your personal qualifications for either assistant or technician.

Currently, technicians' salaries average about $19,739, while those of optometric assistants average $18,150 per year. Ordinarily, your salary will increase rapidly after the first few months on the job.

Job Outlook

What holds true for almost all paramedical fields is true of paraoptometrics, too. Employment prospects look bright primarily because of the nation's aging population and the resulting demand for optometrists' and other medical professionals' services. But increasingly the best job opportunities will go to graduates of accredited training programs for both optometric assistants and optometric technicians.

For More Information

To obtain additional information about this field, write to:

American Optometric Association
  Paraoptometric Section
  243 N. Lindbergh Boulevard
  St. Louis, MO 63141

THE OPHTHALMIC ASSISTANT, TECHNICIAN, AND TECHNOLOGIST

Like paraoptometrics, ophthalmic assistants, technicians, and technologists are paramedicals qualified by their training and experience to perform support services for the medical professional that employs them; in this case, the ophthalmologist. Working under the supervision of the ophthalmologist, they carry out various services involved in the diagnosis and treatment of eye disease.

Although there is some overlapping of duties at the three levels of the paramedicals involved, the duties become increasingly involved and complex as you advance from one level to the next.

On the lowest rung of the ladder is the ophthalmic assistant, followed by the technician, and finally the technologist.

What They Do

As an ophthalmic assistant, the somewhat restricted but nevertheless important tasks that you would handle include but are not limited to:

- measuring visual acuity, with or without eyeglasses
- obtaining the patient's ophthalmic (eye) history, paying special attention to any eye problems or complaints
- obtaining other technical measurements, such as sphere, cylinder, and axis of lenses
- caring for and maintaining eye care equipment
- handling minor adjustments and repairs in eyeglasses and ophthalmalogic instruments

Besides the job functions and services listed above, as an ophthalmic technician you would handle more advanced procedures including:

- measuring for contact lens fittings and instructing patients in the insertion, removal, and care of lenses
- taking eye smears as specimens for eye culture examinations
- making comprehensive measurements for ocular mobility
- handling direct patient care functions including changing of eye dressings, installing eye drops and ointments, administering medications, and instructing patients on home eye care

- performing advanced maintenance functions of ophthalmic instruments and equipment such as optical alignment and calibration

Besides these functions, as an ophthalmic technologist you are trained to perform still other tasks on an even higher level. For example, you might carry out certain clinical procedures within specialized areas of ophthalmology, such as assisting in eye surgery. Other jobs you might be assigned include:

- testing patients with special instruments such as ultrasound diagnostic equipment to determine extent of eye problems
- conducting advanced tests for color vision

Education and Training

To qualify for training in this career, you must at least have a high school diploma. You also should have scientific curiosity, sound judgment, a spirit of cooperativeness, maturity, and the quality of accuracy.

To qualify for a career in ophthalmic medical assisting, you must either have completed on-the-job training or a formal training program.

In 1998, there were twenty-eight recognized and accredited programs in the United States. Programs last from one to two years and include courses in anatomy and physiology, medical terminology, medical law and ethics, ophthalmic optics, and microbiology. The programs also include clinical training such as visual field testing, contact lenses, ophthalmic surgery, and care and maintenance of ophthalmic equipment.

Each program is geared toward one of the three certification levels—that is, for ophthalmic assistant, technician, or technologist—so programs vary in intensity and length. For more information on formal training programs, write to the Joint Commission on Allied

Health Personnel in Ophthalmology. The address is listed at the end of this section.

Certification also can be obtained by working in an ophthalmologist's office, successfully completing an approved home study course, and passing a certifying examination. Passing the initial certification as ophthalmic assistant is required before you can advance to a higher level of certification. Examinations are administered throughout the year at many locations in the United States and Canada.

To maintain certification, you must earn a specific number of JCAHPO-approved continuing education credits, which vary according to the level of certification.

Earnings

What you earn in this field will depend on your level of certification, where you work (in a private office, at a medical school, or in a medical center), the location of the practice, and your own background and experience.

According to the JCAHPO, recent entry-level salaries for assistants began at $20,000 and can go as high as $50,000 or more depending on your certification and where you work. For additional salary information, contact the Association of Technical Personnel in Ophthalmology at the address listed at the end of this section.

Job Outlook

Employment opportunities are excellent in this field. Ophthalmic medical personnel find jobs in a variety of settings where ophthalmologists practice, including private offices, hospital eye clinics, and university ophthalmology departments. Salaries for ophthalmic paramedicals compare favorably with that of all paramedicals as does job satisfaction. With the population continuing to age, the need for eye care is expected to increase and the demand for well-trained ophthalmic medical personnel will continue to expand.

For More Information

For more information about paraophthalmic careers, contact:

Association of Technical Personnel in Ophthalmology
P.O. Box 25036
St. Paul, MN 55125-0036

Joint Commission on Allied Health Personnel in Ophthalmology
2025 Woodlane Drive
St. Paul, MN 55125

THE ORTHOPTIST

Occupying a very special niche in the entire array of paramedicals is the orthoptist. For one, this is a very specialized field—there are only an estimated three hundred persons in the entire field in the United States. Then, too, the demands are very high and the training very intensive. For one, you need a college degree to be admitted.

The focus of this career is the evaluation and treatment of disorders of vision, eye movement, and eye alignment of children and adults. Your primary concern would be treating and diagnosing eye conditions affecting eye mobility and binocular vision (using both eyes at the same time to see). Here, working under the supervision of the ophthalmologist, you would handle primarily children suffering from strabismus, otherwise known as crossed eyes.

You also might be called on to treat an eye condition known as amblyopia (lazy eye), which is most commonly seen in children but affects adults as well.

Education and Certification

To qualify for this career, you must have completed your undergraduate college training. Beyond that, for certification, you must have completed a two-year program in orthoptics accredited by the American Orthoptic Council. With JCAHPO certification as an ophthalmic technician or technologist, you may be able to receive advanced standing status and study for one year, instead of two.

Once you have completed the orthoptic program and passed a written and oral/practical examination given by the council, you may then qualify for certification. Recertification requires proof of continuing education on an annual basis.

To qualify for orthoptic training, you should take courses in biology, anatomy, optics, and child development. The curriculum combines classroom lectures with study of journal publications and of the proceedings of various scientific meetings. The program usually covers anatomy, neuroanatomy, physiology, pharmacology, ophthalmic optics, and diagnostic testing and measurement.

Earnings

As is true of all paramedical careers, your earnings will depend upon where you work—in a private office, public clinic, or a military facility; the section of the country in which you work; and your background and experience.

In recent years, starting salaries for orthoptists have ranged from $19,000 to $23,000 a year, but with experience and proven ability, you can earn well in excess of $50,000 a year.

Job Outlook

This is a field in which the demand for qualified personnel is far outstripping the availability of trained workers. With the aging of the population, which will be reflected in increased demand for optical services, the demand for skilled orthoptists should grow even sharper.

For More Information

For additional information about a career as an orthoptist, write to:

American Orthoptic Council
   3914 Nakoma Road
   Madison, WI 53711

CHAPTER 9

PHYSICAL THERAPIST ASSISTANTS

As is true of just about all medical and healthcare professionals, physical therapists are busy people. To enable them to use their time most effectively and to tend to the needs of ever-increasing numbers of patients, they rely on the paramedical—in this case, the physical therapist assistant.

Don't confuse the *physical therapist assistant* with the *physical therapist aide.* Assistants are for the most part trained in various accredited educational programs, while aides are trained on the job and work under a physical therapist or a physical therapist assistant.

WHAT PHYSICAL THERAPIST ASSISTANTS DO

Ordinarily, the nature and extent of your duties as a physical therapist assistant are determined by the institution where you work and your supervising physical therapist. Generally, the physical therapist is concerned with the diagnosis and evaluation of the patient to be treated, as well as the development of the treatment plan. Such treatment plans often include giving tests to determine loss of muscle strength, motor development, functional ability, capacity for respiration, and circulation efficiency.

Once the treatment plan has been developed, it is your job as physical therapist assistant to carry out the specifics of the plan, including:

- rendering exercises, massages, electrical stimulation, paraffin baths, hot/cold packs, traction, and ultrasound to help patients regain the use of their limbs
- assisting in carrying out and evaluating tests and more complex treatment procedures
- observing and reporting patients' progress
- administering traction to relieve neck and back pain
- using intermittent and stationary traction equipment
- fitting patients for adjustments and training them in the use of orthopedic and supportive devices such as canes, crutches, walkers, and wheelchairs
- orienting new physical therapist assistants to the job
- exchanging information with the physical therapy staff on patient treatment plans, progress, and problems
- handling such clerical duties as taking inventory, ordering supplies, answering the phone, and taking messages
- evaluating patients' range of motion, length and girth of limbs, and vital signs to measure the effectiveness of various treatments or to assist the physical therapist in patient evaluation

EDUCATION AND CERTIFICATION

According to the American Physical Therapy Association, there currently are 225 accredited physical therapist assistant programs in the United States. These programs, which ordinarily run two years, are offered in community and junior colleges, as well as in four-year colleges and universities and at medical centers. The programs are divided between a year of academic study and working with patients during the second year. Academic courses include algebra, geometry, physiology, biology, chemistry, and psychology. Before you can start your clinical work, many schools require that you complete a semester of anatomy and physiology and are certified in CPR and first aid. Admission to physical therapist assistant training programs is very competitive, so you may face a long waiting list to get in. It is therefore desirable that you contact any schools in which you are interested (see Appendix D) for information regarding admission requirements, costs, and any financial assistance available.

In high school, it is highly desirable that you take courses in health, biology, mathematics, psychology, physical education, and computer science.

Licensure or registration is currently required in forty-one states. To qualify for licensure, you must be a graduate of an accredited program and pass a written examination given by the state. But certification requirements do vary from state to state, so it is best that you contact your state licensing board for its specific requirements. Requirements for renewal of certification also varies by state, so be sure to consult your school's career counseling office or the state licensure board.

EARNINGS

Salary information for physical therapist assistants is limited, but in 1996, assistants averaged about $24,000 a year. Salaries for physical therapist assistants were somewhat higher if you worked in private practice and lower if you were employed by a hospital. According to the American Physical Therapy Association, experienced assistants working in private practice averaged about $30,000 a year in 1996. But salaries do vary according to geographical location, the setting in which you work, and, of course, your background and experience.

JOB OUTLOOK

Licensed physical therapist assistants are anticipated to be among the fastest increasing occupations in the next decade. It is estimated that demand for assistants will continue to rise with the increase in persons with handicaps or disabilities or with limited use of their limbs. Elderly persons are especially vulnerable to chronic and debilitating conditions requiring treatment by physical therapists and their assistants. Also seen as a factor in the need for treatment and therapy is the aging of the so-called baby boomers as they approach the age of higher incidence of heart attacks and strokes, thus creating increased need for cardiac and physical treatment. In addition, the increased participation of the population in sports and physical fitness activities will further accelerate the demand for physical therapist assistants to treat and help prevent knee, leg, shoulder, back, and other injuries involving the musculoskeletal system.

FOR MORE INFORMATION

For additional information about this career, contact:

American Physical Therapy Association
1111 N. Fairfax Street
Alexandria, VA 22314-1488

CHAPTER 10

THE OCCUPATIONAL
THERAPY ASSISTANT

In the previous chapter, we described how physical therapist assistants work with the physical therapist in implementing treatment plans to restore their patients' physical functions—walking, use of a hand or foot, neck, and so forth. So physical therapists and assistants are primarily concerned with restoring physical function to the disabled.

Occupational therapy, on the other hand, is concerned with working with patients to help them learn the tasks of everyday living that are required to function as human beings: learning, for example, how to dress and cook for yourself, how to pick up objects, how to button your coat, or how to tie a tie.

As a physical therapist, you might help stroke victims regain their ability to walk. But as an occupational therapist, you are more concerned with teaching those patients how to dress or undress themselves, prepare meals, and take care of their homes while at the same time striving to overcome any temporary bilateral paralysis.

As you can see from this brief description, the occupational therapist has nothing to do with finding a job for the patient, but rather gets that patient to function to the best of his or her ability in the task of everyday living. And as an occupational therapy assistant, you work under the supervision of a registered occupational therapist (OTR) in a variety of tasks and functions, which are described below.

WHAT OCCUPATIONAL THERAPY ASSISTANTS DO

Because you work with such a broad range of patients and illnesses and disabilities, you must as an occupational therapy assistant be able to handle a broad range of tasks including:

- helping a patient to handle self-care tasks such as dressing, eating, washing, and grooming
- working with patients to prepare for job interviews or to attain the tools or skills they need for employment
- helping make splints, braces, and other devices and maintaining tools and equipment
- planning group or individual projects to help patients become independent to the greatest degree possible consistent with their achieving personal satisfaction
- assisting in client evaluation and reporting patient progress and current status to the occupational therapist

Although there are no official specialties in this field, you may end up working primarily with patients with certain kinds of disabilities: stroke, arthritis, diabetes, and so forth.

EDUCATIONAL REQUIREMENTS

To qualify for employment in this field, you must be a graduate of an educational training program for assistants accredited by the American Occupational Therapy Association and then pass a national certification examination.

Programs usually include such courses as human anatomy and physiology, physical and emotional effects of illness and injury, human growth and development, occupational therapy theory, and techniques of treatment and mental development. All programs require that you have three months of supervised field work experience.

If you plan to make occupational therapy assistant your career, you should, besides taking courses in biology in high school, strive to acquire work experience as a volunteer in a health field. With such experience, most schools will give you preference.

Since educational requirements vary from school to school, it is strongly suggested that you write for specific entrance information from the school or schools in which you are interested. Programs are offered at colleges and universities and at vocational, technical, and community colleges throughout the United States (see Appendix E). There are no on-the-job training programs.

CERTIFICATION

Upon completion of an accredited program, you must, as an entry-level Certified Occupational Therapy Assistant (COTA) applicant, pass a national certification examination administered by the National Board for Certification of Occupational Therapy (NBCOT).

SALARIES

A recent salary survey indicated that salaries for certified occupational therapy assistants averaged $31,000 per year. Salaries ranged from $10,000 to $64,000 depending on the level of experience, practice setting (whether you work for a private practice, a hospital, or a government agency), and geographical area.

FUTURE OUTLOOK

According to the Bureau of Labor Statistics, occupational therapists and occupational therapy assistants are projected to be among the ten fastest growing occupations. Because the total number of people employed—estimated at sixteen thousand in 1998—is small, openings will be restricted, but certified assistants should have no trouble finding employment at least for the foreseeable future. Growth will result not only from the coming of age of the so-called baby boomers, but also because of advances in medicine that will allow more people with critical disabilities and injuries to survive and to need rehabilitative therapy.

FOR MORE INFORMATION

For additional information about this career, write:

American Occupational Therapy Association
  4720 Montgomery Lane
  P.O. Box 31220
  Bethesda, MD 20824-1220

CHAPTER 11

PSYCHIATRIC TECHNICIANS

In the preceding chapters, we have focused on those paramedicals concerned primarily with a person's physical or emotional health. But equally important, from the standpoint of the individual's total health picture, is mental health, which affects almost every aspect of our lives: how we react to stress, how we deal with people, and even our physical health and well being. Studies have shown that your mental health can greatly affect your physical health and well being.

In this chapter we focus on paramedicals who work with professionals in the area of mental health in helping patients with mental health problems to attain a higher quality of life. To illustrate how mental health affects qualify of life, you need only consider that if your behavior is constantly being disrupted or upset by feelings of guilt, anger, depression, and fear, you obviously cannot function as well as a healthy, productive human being.

The kinds of treatment called for will depend to a large degree on the severity of the illness or the inability to function. For the more severe mental illnesses, the services of various mental health professionals—psychiatrists and psychologists, psychiatric social workers and psychiatric registered nurses—are called for. Such professionals, who often have eight or more years of postcollege training, are qualified to handle the more complex forms of mental illness.

But working along with them in putting into effect mental health plans and in helping to diagnose and observe the progress of those with mental health problems are psychiatric technicians, also known as mental health technicians, among others. Such paramedicals are qualified to work with other members of the mental health team in diagnosing, observing, and working with the mentally ill.

Here your duties will vary a lot depending on the work setting, but your assignment may include helping patients with hygiene and housekeeping and recording patients' pulse, temperature, and respiration. Often you may be called on to take part in treatment programs in a one-to-one session with patients, under a nurse's or counselor's supervision.

Another important assignment is recording your observations of patients' behavior to other members of the mental health team. In other cases you may fill out admitting forms for new patients, contact patients' families for conferences, issue medications from the pharmacy, and maintain records.

Today, many psychiatric technicians are trained in two-year associate degree programs, most of which are offered under various labels, depending on their emphasis. Many are categorized as human service programs, because their graduates, though they might be considered psychiatric technicians, are qualified to work with the mentally ill in various settings, all of which provide human services.

WHAT PSYCHIATRIC TECHNICIANS DO

Usually the specific services and functions of psychiatric technicians are part of a broad treatment plan worked out by the supervising psychiatrist and other mental health professionals.

Psychiatric technicians should not be confused with psychiatric aides, who may perform some of the same duties. In general, as a psychiatric technician, you receive much more extensive training and are qualified to assume greater responsibilities than a psychiatric aide. Although the latter may work with patients in daily activities, exercises, and so forth, their training program is too short to qualify as a paramedical as outlined in Chapter 1 of this book. They are, therefore, not included in our discussion.

As a psychiatric technician you participate both in the planning and implementing of individual patient treatment plans. Specific duties vary according to where you work, but may include most of the following tasks in a hospital unit:

- admitting, screening, evaluating, and discharging patients
- interviewing and gathering information for the patient's records
- participating in individual and group counseling and therapy sessions
- referring patients to community agencies
- visiting patients in their homes after they are discharged
- handling recordkeeping
- working with patients in behavior modification and development of social skills

In addition, in a hospital setting, you might be called on to perform certain general nursing functions:

- taking temperatures, pulse counts, blood pressures, and respiration rates
- observing various aspects of patients' lives, including eating, sleeping, and personal hygiene

If you work in a clinic, halfway house, or community mental health center, your duties might include, in addition to those listed above, some that are unique to these settings:

- interviewing newly registered patients and their families
- visiting patients and families at home
- participating in group activities
- administering psychological tests
- reviewing patients' progress for supervising psychiatrists and other mental health professionals

Although you most likely would work as a generalist in this career, there are opportunities to specialize in certain areas of mental health care. You might, for instance, work with mentally disturbed children, as a counselor in a drug or alcohol abuse program, or as a member of a psychiatric emergency or crisis intervention team.

In a community health clinic, your major concerns might indeed be in working with victims of drug or alcohol abuse, parental abuse, or working with the elderly. With some training modification, you might specialize in the treatment of the mentally retarded.

In addition to these functions, the *Federal Dictionary of Occupational Titles* notes that duties of a psychiatric technician include administering oral medications and hypodermic injections and intervening to restrain violent or potentially violent or suicidal patients either by ordering them to desist or by taking whatever physical action is required.

EDUCATIONAL REQUIREMENTS

At the very least you must have a high school diploma to find work as a psychiatric technician, although in most cases you are expected to have at least two years of post–high school training. And many hospitals now prefer that you have a bachelor's degree before they will hire you. You should find out as soon as possible the admissions requirements of schools in which you are interested. In high school, useful courses include English, biology, psychology, and sociology.

The two-year post–high school educational programs lead to an associate of arts or associate of science degree. Study programs include such courses as human development, the nature of mental illness, personality structure, and, to a limited degree, anatomy, physiology, basic nursing, and medical science. Other subjects frequently offered include an introduction to basic social sciences, to give you a better understanding of family and community structure, an overview of the structure and function of institutions that treat patients, and practical training to familiarize you with the skills that you will need in this field.

On the average, most programs offer about a fourth general study courses such as English, sociology, and psychology; a fourth courses in mental-health-related courses, such as the family and social welfare institutions, early childhood development, and general and abnormal psychology; and still another fourth in such specific areas as psychopathology, prevention techniques, and forms of therapy and rehabilitation, general and psychiatric nursing. The final fourth of the training offers students practical and field learning experiences.

CERTIFICATION

In Colorado, California, Kansas, and Arkansas you must be licensed to work in this field. But in other states certification is optional. You should consult your guidance or placement counselor in school, prior to graduation, for more information about certification requirements in your state. Such certification is available through the American Association of Psychiatric Technicians (its address is listed at the end of this chapter).

There are in general four levels of certification, each with increasingly higher requirements. At level 1, you must have a high school diploma and pass a written examination. For certification at level 2, you must have thirty semester hours of credit, a year's practical experience, and pass a written test. For level 3 certification, you must have an associate's degree, two years of practical experience, and pass a written exam. Finally, for level 4 certification, you must have a bachelor's degree, three years of experience, and again pass a written exam.

Although currently only a few states require certification, the trend is toward requiring such certification, and would-be psychiatric technicians are urged to obtain such certification even if still optional in your state.

EARNINGS

According to the American Association of Psychiatric Technicians, most technicians are paid by the hour, and in 1998, earnings in this field ranged from $7 to $12 per hour, with some technicians earning as much as $15 per hour. With increased experience, you can expect some modest increase in salary; some senior psychiatric technicians earn as much as $27,000 per year. Salaries vary according to geographical area and work setting, with earnings the highest in California and if you work in a state mental hospital.

In most cases, you can expect to receive some fringe benefits, including hospitalization insurance, sick leave, and paid vacations.

FUTURE OUTLOOK

As is true of nearly all paramedical fields, the employment outlook for psychiatric technicians is good, due primarily to two factors: There is an increasingly strong trend to return hospitalized patients to their homes following ever increasingly shorter hospital stays. This in turn has encouraged development of comprehensive community mental health centers and boosted the need for trained psychiatric technicians.

Then, too, increasing concerns over ever-accelerating health care costs should increase job opportunities in this field since psychiatric technicians can assume many of the functions of higher-paid professionals.

FOR MORE INFORMATION

For further information about this career, contact:

American Association of Psychiatric Technicians
2059 S. Third Street
Niles, MI 49120

American Psychiatric Association
1400 K Street, NW
Washington, DC 20005

CHAPTER 12

THE OUTLOOK FOR PARAMEDICAL CAREERS

In general, as has been shown throughout this book, jobs for paramedicals are expected to increase much more sharply than is true of the population as a whole. Because of the strong demand for personnel trained as paramedicals, the past thirty-five years have witnessed a huge growth in the number of paramedicals employed.

In just a few decades, the number of paramedicals has gone from a small band of paramedics and largely untrained physician assistants to an army hundreds of thousands strong—medical assistants alone account for more than 200,000 paramedicals. In addition there are more than fifty fields in which paramedicals are employed. Most of these new fields now have their own professional associations and standards for licensure and certification, which are required in many states, as well as standards for accreditation of training programs.

Despite this vast expansion, predicting the trends in paramedical careers for the next thirty years in such areas as training, licensure, certification, and employment is risky. Even so, it seems fairly certain that for the next decade or so, opportunities for paramedicals will be especially promising, for reasons listed below.

NEW TRENDS IN PARAMEDICAL CAREERS

In Chapter 2, we saw that there are several trends that have fueled the increased demand and use of paramedical workers—for one, the continuing aging of the population, with a corresponding need for health services. After all, those over sixty-five are the heaviest users of healthcare services, and it follows that the demand for medical and health services should accelerate as the population ages.

Then, too, it's a fact that vast numbers of our citizens are now covered by insurance—both private and public. Only about four decades ago, the bulk of Americans, estimated at more than 90 percent, paid for medical and health care services out of their own pockets. Today, such programs as Medicare and Medicaid, and other federally sponsored health programs and private insurance plans, including HMOs, pick up more than 50 percent of the healthcare bill. Healthcare services today are available to most of us, as never before.

Along with this expansion of coverage has come an increased awareness of new discoveries in medicine and healthcare on the part of our citizens through increased coverage being given healthcare services by the news media. Today, it is increasingly common to see or hear reporters specializing in medicine and healthcare on the radio or TV or in newspapers and magazines. Increasingly we are learning of new discoveries in the diagnosis and treatment of disease almost as these are announced, and we are demanding these new services from our doctors.

As a result of this demand for healthcare services and a corresponding shortage of physicians, nurses, and other healthcare professionals, Americans spent more than $884 billion on health care, approximately 11 percent of the gross national product in 1993. Healthcare is the fastest growing part of the GNP, far outstripping food, shelter, and transportation. Because of these runaway healthcare costs, the government has adopted a multifaceted program aimed at braking these costs, which we need not go into in this limited space. But as a result of these efforts on the part of the federal government and to a lesser degree private industry, hospital stays are shorter today, and admissions have been cut down to those found to require short-term acute care. These cost-cutting efforts in turn have prompted healthcare providers such as hospitals, nursing homes, and private clinics to try to cut costs to an ever-increasing degree.

And certainly one of the most effective ways to do this is by increasing the number of paramedicals. Take the paramedical field of physician assistant (see Chapter 3). It is estimated that the physician assistant can now handle an estimated 80 to 90 percent of the patients treated by the family practitioner, but they can do so at a savings of more than 50 percent since they earn less than 50 percent of the salary of the family practitioner.

In so doing, they are helping to alleviate the shortage of family practitioners, internists, and other primary care physicians, which have until comparatively recently failed to attract the number of medical graduates that the more lucrative fields of cardiovascular and plastic surgery, radiology, and other such specialties do.

The federal government has taken yet additional steps to bring down costs. These include prospective payments (made in anticipation of actual costs) through Diagnosis Related Groups (DRGs). Here the government pays hospitals and other healthcare providers just so much for a wide variety of illnesses and diagnoses. If providers can keep costs of healthcare services under the amount allotted in the DRG, they can make a profit, but if costs exceed the funds allotted, the providers must absorb the additional costs.

Little wonder then why, under these circumstances, healthcare providers have added paramedicals to their staffs in record numbers. They will continue this trend in the foreseeable future in ever-accelerating numbers since the emphasis on cost cutting is expected to continue well into the new century.

Then, too, increased specialization has created a growing number of new medical and professional specialties requiring a year or more of postgraduate education. This becomes readily apparent by the American Medical Association's Committee on Allied Health Education and Accreditation (COAHEA), which currently accredits forty-seven allied health careers. Included in these careers are such fields as perfusionist, radiologic technologist, cytotechnologist, and others, which are among the fastest growing of all healthcare fields. Since those employed in these careers do not ordinarily work directly with doctors or other healthcare professionals, nor do they otherwise fit our definition of paramedicals as outlined in Chapter 1, we have not included them in this book.

EMPLOYMENT OPPORTUNITIES

For all of the reasons listed above—including need by healthcare providers to cut costs; shortage of qualified healthcare professionals, especially primary care physicians, but others as well; plus the increased demand for healthcare services fueled by the aging of the population—the need for qualified paramedicals is expected to increase sharply in the next decade. The Department of Labor lists paramedical careers such as dental assistants and dental hygienists, emergency medical technicians, medical assistants, occupational therapy assistants, and physical therapist assistants among the fastest growing occupations and those anticipated to show the greatest numerical increase in employment by 2006. For example, physical therapist assistants are expected to show an 82 percent increase in the number of those employed, and medical assistants an increase of approximately 78 percent followed by occupational therapy assistants with a 70 percent increase in employment, dental hygienists with a 45 percent increase, and physician assistants with a 44 percent increase.

EDUCATION AND TRAINING

As the paramedical career fields become more established, training programs are expected to become more professionalized to ensure that graduates meet the required standards. Increasingly, training programs in many paramedical fields are becoming lengthier, and they are being offered in academic settings rather than as part of hospital training programs. This is especially true of advanced practice nurses, such as nurse practitioners, nurse anesthetists, and nurse midwives (see Chapter 3).

Accompanying this increase in standards of training programs is an increase in the standards for certification or licensing required to pursue paramedical careers by professional organizations and state licensing boards. And increasingly coming into play are new and more demanding standards for continuing education as a means of remaining accredited. Such continuing education standards are being developed and updated in many paramedical fields as a means of keeping personnel up to par. This trend for higher standards of continuing education can be expected to grow in the near future.

Many professional paramedical associations are already requiring that members adhere to standards for continuing education; more can be expected to develop such standards to make sure that paramedicals covered can meet employer requirements.

The overall effect of these trends would seem to result in paramedicals who are better trained and more able to take on new responsibilities.

PARAMEDICAL VERSATILITY IN DEMAND

This recognition of the importance of increased skills and capabilities has in recent years seen a corresponding trend toward graduating paramedicals with skills in more than one area.

Although this trend is perhaps more marked in technological fields than in the paramedical area, there is nevertheless a definite trend toward more specialization and versatility. To keep hospital costs down while providing quality healthcare services, hospitals and other healthcare providers (group clinics, group practices, and medical centers, among others) are looking to paramedicals to handle an ever-expanding variety of primary care and secondary functions. This new emphasis will in turn result in training programs more attuned to providing students with skills that enable them to handle newer and expanded duties.

ACCREDITED EDUCATIONAL PROGRAMS

The following appendixes contain lists of various paramedical training programs that have been accredited by the American Medical Association. These training programs will get you started in your paramedical career. For further information, consult the *1998–1999 Health Professions Education Directory,* a comprehensive compilation of more than five thousand educational programs spanning the forty-seven most prominent healthcare fields. This directory contains all of the information you will need to choose the program that is right for you, including contact names and numbers, educational and admissions standards, tuition, and salary and occupational outlooks for the various professions. To obtain a copy of this directory, contact:

American Medical Association
   Medical Education Products
   515 N. State Street
   Chicago, IL 60610
   800-621-8335
   Fax: 312-464-3830

PHYSICIAN ASSISTANT TRAINING PROGRAMS

Alabama

University of Alabama at Birmingham
  Surgeon Assistant Prgm.
  Sch. of Hlth. Related Professions
  1715 Ninth Ave. S/ UAB Station
  Birmingham, AL 35294-1270
  Tel: 205-934-4407 *Fax:* 205-975-7302
  E-mail: geraldj@admin.shrp.uab.edu

University of Southern Alabama
  Physician Assistant Prgm.
  Dept. of Physician Asst. Studies
  1504 Springhill Ave./Ste. 4410
  Mobile, AL 36604-3273
  Tel: 334-434-3641 *Fax:* 334-434-3646

Arizona

Arizona School of Health Science
  Physician Assistant Prgm.
  3210 W. Camelback Rd.
  Phoenix, AZ 85017-1037
  Tel: 602-841-4077 *Fax:* 602-841-4092
  E-mail: rdavis@az/swc.kcom.edu

California

Charles R. Drew Univ. of Medicine &
    Science
  Physician Assistant Prgm.
  1621 E. 120th St./MP #42
  Los Angeles, CA 90059-3025
  Tel: 213-563-5879 *Fax:* 213-563-4833
  E-mail: belassit@cdrewu.edu

University of Southern California
  Physician Assistant Prgm.
  Health Sciences Campus
  1975 Zonal Park/KAM-B29
  Los Angeles, CA 90033-1039
  Tel: 213-342-1328 *Fax:* 213-342-1260
  E-mail: skern@hsc.usc.edu

Stanford University School of
    Medicine
  Physician Assistant Prgm.
  Primary Care Associate Prgm.
  703 Welch Rd., Ste. G-1
  Palo Alto, CA 94304-1760
  Tel: 415-723-7043

Western Univ. of Health Sciences
  Physician Assistant Prgm.
  Primary Care
  450 E. Second St.
  College Plaza
  Pomona, CA 91766-1889
  Tel: 909-469-5390 *Fax:* 909-629-7255

University of California–Davis
  Physician Assistant Prgm.
  2525 Stockton Blvd./Ste. 1025
  Sacramento, CA 95817
  Tel: 916-734-3550 *Fax:* 916-452-2112
  E-mail: carol.cash@
    ucdmc.ucdavis.edu

Colorado

University of Colorado Health Science
    Center
  Physician Assistant Prgm.
  Child Hlth. Assoc. Prgm.
  4200 E. Ninth.Ave./ P.O. Box C219
  Denver, CO 80262
  Tel: 303-315-7963 *Fax:* 303-315-6976
  E-mail: gerald.merenstein@uchsc.edu

Connecticut

Quinnipiac College
  Physician Assistant Prgm.
  275 Mt. Carmel Ave.
  Hamden, CT 06518
  Tel: 203-281-8983 *Fax:* 203-287-5303

Yale University School of Medicine
  Physician Assistant Prgm.
  47 College St., Ste. 220
  New Haven, CT 06510
  Tel: 203-785-4252
  E-mail: elaine.grant@ yale.edu

District of Columbia

George Washington University
  Physician Assistant Prgm.
  2175 K St./Ste. 820
  Washington, DC 20037
  Tel: 202-530-2393 *Fax:* 202-530-2360
  E-mail: gwu_pa@gwis2.circ.gwu.edu

Howard University
    Physician Assistant Prgm.
    Sixth & Bryant Sts. NW
    Washington, DC 20060
    Tel: 202-806-7536 *Fax:* 202-806-4476

Florida

Nova Southeastern University
    Physician Assistant Prgm.
    3200 S. University Dr.
    Ft. Lauderdale, FL 33328
    Tel: 954-626-1650 *Fax:* 954-916-2285
    E-mail: davidz@hpd.acast.
        nova.edu

University of Florida
    Physician Assistant Prgm.
    College of Medicine
    P.O. Box 100176
    Gainesville, FL 32610-0176
    Tel: 352-395-7955 *Fax:* 352-395-7996
    E-mail: ops2.pa@shands.ufl.edu

Barry University
    Physician Assistant Prgm.
    11300 NE Second Ave.
    Miami Shores, FL 33161
    Tel: 305-899-3260 *Fax:* 305-899-3253

Georgia

Emory University
    Physician Assistant Prgm.
    School of Medicine
    1462 Clifton Rd./Ste. 280
    Atlanta, GA 30322
    Tel: 404-727-7825 *Fax:* 404-727-7836
    E-mail: vjoslin@pa.emory.edu

Medical College of Georgia
    Physician Assistant Prgm.
    1120 Fifteenth St./AE 1032
    Augusta, GA 30912
    Tel: 706-721-3246 *Fax:* 706-721-3990
    E-mail: bdadig@mail.mcg.edu

South College
    Physician Assistant Prgm.
    709 Mall Blvd.
    Savannah, GA 31406
    Tel: 912-691-6024 *Fax:* 912-691-6082

Idaho

Idaho State University
    Physician Assistant Prgm.
    Campus Box 8253/9195 8th
    Pocatello, ID 83209
    Tel: 208-236-3660 *Fax:* 208-236-4969

Illinois

Southern Illinois University at
        Carbondale
    Physician Assistant Prgm.
    Health Care Professions
    Lindegren Hall/Rm. 129
    Carbondale, IL 62901-6616
    Tel: 618-453-1151 *Fax:* 618-453-7216

Malcolm X Hospital/Cook County
        Hospital
    Physician Assistant Prgm.
    1900 W. Van Buren St./ Room 3234
    Chicago, IL 60612
    Tel: 312-850-7268

Midwestern University
    Physician Assistant Prgm.
    555 Thirty-First St.
    Downers Grove, IL 60515
    Tel: 630-515-6034

Finch University of Health Science/
        Chicago Medical School
    Physician Assistant Prgm.
    3333 Green Bay Rd./Bldg. 51
    North Chicago, IL 60064
    Tel: 847-578-8689 *Fax:* 847-578-8690
    E-mail: knottp@mis.
        finchems.edu

Indiana

Lutheran College of Health Professions
    Physician Assistant Prgm.
    3024 Fairfield Ave.
    Ft. Wayne, IN 46807-1697
    Tel: 219-458-2483 *Fax:* 219-458-3077

Butler University/Methodist Hospital
        of Indiana
    Physician Assistant Prgm.
    Butler Univ. Coll. of Pharm. and Hlth.
        Sci.
    4600 Sunset Ave.
    Indianapolis, IN 46208-3485
    Tel: 317-940-9728 *Fax:* 317-940-6172
    E-mail: pylitt@butler.edu

Iowa

University of Osteopathic Medicine
  Physician Assistant Prgm.
  3200 Grand Ave.
  Des Moines, IA 50312
  Tel: 515-271-1415 *Fax:* 515-271-1543
  E-mail: jcanalan@uomhs.edu

University of Iowa
  Physician Assistant Prgm.
  School of Medicine
  2333 Steindler Building
  Iowa City, IA 52242
  Tel: 319-335-8922 *Fax:* 319-335-8923
  E-mail: david-asprey@uiowa.edu

Kansas

Wichita State University
  Physician Assistant Prgm.
  Campus Box 43/1845 Fairmont
  Wichita, KS 67260
  Tel: 316-978-3011 *Fax:* 316-978-3025
  E-mail: lary@chp.twsu.edu

Kentucky

University of Kentucky Chandler
    Medical Center
  Physician Assistant Prgm.
  Dept. of Health Services
  121 Washington Ave., Rm. 103 CAHP
    Bldg.
  Lexington, KY 40536-0003
  Tel: 606-323-1100, ext 292
  Fax: 606-257-2454

Louisiana

Louisiana State University Medical
    Center–Shreveport
  Physician Assistant Prgm.
  1501 Kings Hwy./ P.O. Box 33932
  Shreveport, LA 71130
  Tel: 318-675-7317 *Fax:* 318-675-6937
  E-mail: vvalgo@mail-sh.lsumc.edu

Maine

University of New England
  Physician Assistant Prgm.
  Gregory Hall Annex, Ste. 4
  11 Hills Beach Rd.
  Biddeford, ME 04005-9599
  Tel: 207-283-0171, ext. 2812
  Fax: 207-282-6379
  E-mail: ctoney@mailbox.une.edu

Maryland

Anne Arundel Community College
  Physician Assistant Prgm.
  101 College Pkwy.
  Arnold, MD 21012
  Tel: 410-541-7310 *Fax:* 410-315-7099

Essex Community College
  Physician Assistant Prgm.
  7201 Rossville Blvd.
  Baltimore, MD 21237
  Tel: 410-780-6579

Massachusetts

Northeastern University
  Physician Assistant Prgm.
  360 Huntington Ave./202 Robinson
  Boston, MA 02115
  Tel: 617-373-3195 *Fax:* 617-373-3338
  E-mail: sgreenberg@lynx. neu.edu

Springfield College
  Physician Assistant Prgm.
  263 Alden St.
  Springfield, MA 01109
  Tel: 413-788-2420 *Fax:* 413-739-5211
  E-mail: spfldcol.edu

Michigan

Grand Valley State University
  Physician Assistant Prgm.
  1 Campus Dr.
  328 Henry Hall
  Allendale, MI 49401
  Tel: 616-895-2735 *Fax:* 616-895-3350

University of Detroit Mercy
  Physician Assistant Prgm.
  8200 W. Outer Dr.
  Detroit, MI 48219
  Tel: 313-993-6057 *Fax:* 313-986-1761
  E-mail: warnismk@udmery. edu

Wayne State University
  Physician Assistant Prgm.
  Coll. of Pharmacy and Allied Hlth.
    Profs.
  428 Shapero Hall
  Detroit, MI 48202
  Tel: 313-577-1368 *Fax:* 313-577-2033

Western Michigan University
  Physician Assistant Prgm.
  Kalamazoo, MI 49008
  Tel: 616-387-2638

Central Michigan University
  Physician Assistant Prgm.
  101 Foust Hall
  Mt. Pleasant, MI 48859
  Tel: 517-774-2478 *Fax:* 517-774-2433

Minnesota

Augsburg College
  Physician Assistant Prgm.
  2211 Riverside Ave./CB 149
  Minneapolis, MN 55454
  Tel: 612-330-1331 *Fax:* 612-330-1757

Missouri

St. Louis University Health Sciences
    Center
  Physician Assistant Prgm.
  1504 S. Grand Blvd./Rm. 401
  St. Louis, MO 63104
  Tel: 314-577-8521 *Fax:* 314-577-8503

Montana

Rocky Mountain College
  Physician Assistant Prgm.
  1511 Poly Dr.
  Billings, MT 59102
  Tel: 406-657-1190 *Fax:* 406-657-1194

Nebraska

Union College
  Physician Assistant Prgm.
  3800 S. Forty-Eighth St.
  Libncoln, NE 68506
  Tel: 402-486-2527 *Fax:* 402-486-2895

University of Nebraska Medical Center
  Physician Assistant Prgm.
  600 S. Forty-Second St.
  Omaha, NE 68198-4300
  Tel: 402-559-7953 *Fax:* 402-559-5356

New Jersey

Seton Hall/University of Medicine &
    Dentistry of New Jersey
  Physician Assistant Prgm.
  65 Bergen St.
  Newark, NJ 07107-3001
  Tel: 973-972-5954 *Fax:* 973-972-7157
  E-mail: thornton@umdnj. edu

University of Medicine and Dentistry
    of New Jersey
  Physician Assistant Prgm.
  Robert Wood Johnson Medical School
  675 Hoes Ln.
  Piscataway, NJ 08854
  Tel: 732-235-4444 *Fax:* 732-235-4820

New Mexico

University of New Mexico School of
    Medicine
  Physician Assistant Prgm.
  Dept. of Family and Community
    Medicine
  2400 Tucker NE
  Albuquerque, NM 87131
  Tel: 505-272-9678 *Fax:* 505-272-9828

New York

Hudson Valley Community College
  Physician Assistant Prgm.
  Albany Medical College A-4
  47 New Scotland Ave.
  Albany, NY 12208
  Tel: 518-262-5251 *Fax:* 518-262-6698
  E-mail: bauersal@office. hvcc.edu

Daemen College
  Physician Assistant Prgm.
  4380 Main St.
  Amherst, NY 14226-3592
  Tel: 716-839-8551 *Fax:* 716-839-8252

Bronx Lebanon Hospital Center
  Physician Assistant Prgm.
  1650 Selwyn Ave./Ste. 11D
  Bronx, NY 10457
  Tel: 718-960-1255 *Fax:* 718-960-1329

SUNY Health Science
    Center–Brooklyn
  Physician Assistant Prgm.
  450 Clarkson Ave./ P.O. Box 1222
  Brooklyn, NY 11203
  Tel: 718-270-2324 *Fax:* 718-270-7459

The Brooklyn Hospital/Long Island
    University
  Physician Assistant Prgm.
  121 DeKalb Avenue
  Brooklyn, NY 11201
  Tel: 718-250-8144 *Fax:* 718-797-1598

D'Youville College
  Physician Assistant Prgm.
  320 Porter Ave.
  Buffalo, NY 14201
  Tel: 716-881-7607 *Fax:* 716-881-7732

Touro College–Dix Hills
  Physician Assistant Prgm.
  Barry Z. Levine School Health
    Sciences
  135 Carman Rd./Bldg. 14
  Dix Hills, NY 11746
  Tel: 516-673-3200 *Fax:* 516-271-7082

Catholic Medical Center of Brooklyn
    & Queens, Inc.
  Physician Assistant Prgm.
  175-05 Horace Harding Expressway
  Fresh Meadows, NY 11365
  Tel: 718-357-0500 *Fax:* 718-357-4588

City College of New York/CUNY
    Medical School
  Physician Assistant Prgm.
  506 Lenox Ave./WP Rm. 619
  New York, NY 10037
  Tel: 212-939-2525 *Fax:* 212-939-2529
  E-mail: ssrbh@cunyvm.cuny.edu

Cornell University Medical College
  Physician Assistant Prgm.
  1300 York Ave./Rm. F-1906
  New York, NY 10021
  Tel: 212-746-5021 *Fax:* 212-746-8680

Rochester Institute of Technology
  Physician Assistant Prgm.
  85 Lamb Memorial Dr.
  Rochester, NY 14623-5604
  Tel: 716-475-5945 *Fax:* 716-475-5766
  E-mail: sjtscl@rit.edu

Bayley Seton Hospital
  Physician Assistant Prgm.
  Bay St. and Vanderbilt Ave.
  Staten Island, NY 10304
  Tel: 718-354-5570 *Fax:* 718-354-6146

Wagner College
  Physician Assistant Prgm.
  Staten Island University Hospital
  74 Melville St.
  Staten Island, NY 10309
  Tel: 718-226-2452 *Fax:* 718-226-2464

SUNY Health Science Center at Stony
    Brook
  Physician Assistant Prgm.
  SHTM-HSC/L2-052
  Stony Brook, NY 11794-8202
  Tel: 516-444-3190 *Fax:* 516-444-7621
  E-mail: plombardo@epo.hsc.
    sunysb.edu

Le Moyne College
  Physician Assistant Prgm.
  Le Moyne Heights
  Syracuse, NY 13214-1399
  Tel: 315-445-4144 *Fax:* 315-445-4787

North Carolina

Duke University Medical Center
  Physician Assistant Prgm.
  P.O. Box 3848
  Durham, NC 27710
  Tel: 919-681-3156 *Fax:* 919-681-3371
  E-mail: carte001@mc.duke.edu

Methodist College
  Physician Assistant Prgm.
  5400 Ramsey St.
  Fayetteville, NC 28311
  Tel: 910-630-7495 *Fax:* 910-630-7218

East Carolina University
  Physician Assistant Prgm.
  School of Allied Health Sciences
  300 Carol Belk Bldg.
  Greenville, NC 27858-4353
  Tel: 919-328-4423 *Fax:* 919-328-4470
  E-mail: huechtkere@mail.ecu.edu

Bowman Gray School of Medicine
  Physician Assistant Prgm.
  Medical Ctr. Blvd.
  Winston-Salem, NC 27157-1006
  Tel: 910-716-4356 *Fax:* 910-716-4432

North Dakota

University of North Dakota School of
    Medicine and Health Science
  Physician Assistant Prgm.
  Div. of Hlth. Practitioners
  Minot State Univ. Campus
  Minot, ND 58707
  Tel: 701-857-3017 *Fax:* 701-777-2389

Ohio

Kettering College of Medical Arts
  Physician Assistant Prgm.
  3737 Southern Blvd.
  Kettering, OH 45429
  Tel: 513-296-7238 *Fax:* 513-297-8130

Cuyahoga Community College
  Physician Assistant Prgm.
  11000 Pleasant Valley Rd.
  Parma, OH 44130
  Tel: 216-987-5123 *Fax:* 216-987-5050
  E-mail: joyce.janicek@tri-c.cc.oh.us

Medical College of Ohio
  Physician Assistant Prgm.
  3000 Arlington Ave.
  Toledo, OH 43614
  Tel: 419-381-4637 *Fax:* 419-381-3051
  E-mail: amiller@magnum.mco.edu

Oklahoma

University of Oklahoma Health
    Sciences Center
  Physician Assistant Prgm.
  P.O. Box 26901
  Oklahoma City, OK 73190
  Tel: 405-271-2058 *Fax:* 405-271-3621

Oregon

Pacific University
  Physician Assistant Prgm.
  2043 College Way
  Forest Grove, OR 97116
  Tel: 503-359-2761 *Fax:* 503-359-2977

Oregon Health Sciences University
  Physician Assistant Prgm.
  3181 SW Sam Jackson Park Rd./GH
    219
  Portland, OR 97201
  Tel: 503-494-1484 *Fax:* 503-494-1409
  E-mail: ruback@ohsu.edu

Pennsylvania

Allentown College of St. Francis de
    Sales
  Physician Assistant Prgm.
  2755 Station Ave.
  Center Valley, PA 18034-9568
  Tel: 610-282-1100, ext. 1474
  Fax: 610-282-2059

Gannon University
  Physician Assistant Prgm.
  109 University Square
  Erie, PA 16541
  Tel: 814-871-5452 *Fax:* 814-871-5662

Seton Hill College
  Physician Assistant Prgm.
  Seton Hill Dr.
  Greensburg, PA 15601
  Tel: 412-830-1097 *Fax:* 412-830-4611

Beaver College
  Physician Assistant Prgm.
  450 S. Easton Rd.
  Glenside, PA 19038
  Tel: 215-572-2082 *Fax:* 215-881-8746

Lock Haven University
  Physician Assistant Prgm.
  401 N. Fairview St.
  G22 Stevenson Library
  Lock Haven, PA 17745
  Tel: 717-893-2168 *Fax:* 717-893-2540

Saint Francis College
  Physician Assistant Prgm.
  Sullivan Hall/Rm. 104
  Loretto, PA 15940
  Tel: 814-472-3131 *Fax:* 814-472-3137
  E-mail: bsimon@sfcpa.edu

Allegheny University of the Health
    Sciences
  Physician Assistant Prgm.
  1505 Race St./8th Fl.
  Philadelphia, PA 19102
  Tel: 215-762-7349 *Fax:* 215-762-1164
  E-mail: stolbergs@allegheny.edu

Philadelphia College of Textiles and
    Science
  Physician Assistant Prgm.
  School of Science and Health
  School House Ln. and Henry Ave.
  Philadelphia, PA 19144
  Tel: 215-951-2908 *Fax:* 215-951-2651

Chatham College
  Physician Assistant Prgm.
  Woodland Rd.
  Pittsburgh, PA 15232
  Tel: 412-365-1412 *Fax:* 412-365-1213
  E-mail: allison@chatham.edu

Duquesne University
  Physician Assistant Prgm.
  Rangos School of Health Sciences
  Health Sciences Bldg./Rm. 122
  Pittsburgh, PA 15282-0001
  Tel: 412-396-5914 *Fax:* 412-396-5554
  E-mail: pinevich@duq2.cc.duq.edu

King's College
  Physician Assistant Prgm.
  133 N. River St.
  Wilkes Barre, PA 18711
  Tel: 717-826-5853 *Fax:* 717-826-5353
  E-mail: erbaroni@kssoo2

Pennsylvania College of Technology
  Physician Assistant Prgm.
  One College Ave./#123
  Williamsport, PA 17701
  Tel: 717-327-4779 *Fax:* 717-327-4527
  E-mail: rtrapp@pct.edu

South Carolina

Medical University of South Carolina
  Physician Assistant Prgm.
  171 Ashley Ave.
  Charleston, SC 29425
  Tel: 803-792-6490 *Fax:* 803-792-0506
  E-mail: metzae@musc.edu

South Dakota

University of South Dakota
  Physician Assistant Prgm.
  414 E. Clark St.
  Vermillion, SD 57069
  Tel: 605-677-5128 *Fax:* 605-677-6569
  E-mail: gstewart@sunflowr. usd.edu

Tennessee

Trevecca Nazarene University
  Physician Assistant Prgm.
  333 Murfreesboro Rd.
  Nashville, TN 37210-2877
  Tel: 615-248-1225 *Fax:* 615-248-1622
  E-mail: dlennon@ trevecca.edu

Texas

University of Texas Southwestern
    Medical Center–Dallas
  Physician Assistant Prgm.
  5323 Harry Hines Blvd.
  Dallas, TX 75235-9090
  Tel: 214-648-1701 *Fax:* 214-648-1003
  E-mail: ejones@mednet.swmed.edu

Academy of Health Sciences
    Interservice Training Review
    Organization
  Interservice Physician Assistant Prgm.
  MCCS HMP (PA Br.)
  Ft. Sam Houston, TX 78234-6138
  Tel: 210-221-6863 *Fax:* 210-221-8493

University of North Texas Health
    Science Center at Ft. Worth
  Physician Assistant Prgm.
  3500 Camp Bowie Blvd.
  Ft. Worth, TX 76107
  Tel: 817-735-2301 *Fax:* 817-735-2529

University of Texas Medical Branch
  Physician Assistant Prgm.
  301 University Blvd.
  Galveston, TX 77555-1028
  Tel: 409-772-3046 *Fax:* 409-772-9710
  E-mail: rrahr%sahs@mhost.utmb.edu

Baylor College of Medicine
  Physician Assistant Prgm.
  One Baylor Plaza
  Houston, TX 77030
  Tel: 713-798-4619 *Fax:* 713-798-6128
  E-mail: rosemary@bcm. tmc.edu

Utah

University of Utah Health Sciences
    Center
  Physician Assistant Prgm.
  50 N. Medical Dr./Bldg. 528
  Salt Lake City, UT 84132
  Tel: 801-581-7764 *Fax:* 801-581-5807
  E-mail: dpedersen@upap. utah.edu

Virginia

College of Health Sciences
  Physician Assistant Prgm.
  P.O. Box 13186
  Roanoke, VA 24031-3186
  Tel: 540-985-4016 *Fax:* 540-985-9773
  E-mail: southard@health.chs.edu

Washington

University of Washington
  Physician Assistant Prgm.
  MEDEX Northwest
  4245 Roosevelt Way NE
  Seattle, WA 98105-6920
  Tel: 206-548-2600 *Fax:* 206-548-5195
  E-mail: rballweg@u.
    washington.edu

West Virginia

College of West Virginia
  Physician Assistant Prgm.
  P.O. Box AG
  Beckley, WV 25802
  Tel: 304-253-7351, ext. 420
  Fax: 304-253-0789

Alderson–Broaddus College
  Physician Assistant Prgm.
  P.O. Box 578
  500 College Hill Dr.
  Philippi, WV 26416
  Tel: 304-457-6290 *Fax:* 304-457-6308
  E-mail: holt_m@ab.edu

Wisconsin

University of Wisconsin–LaCrosse
  Physician Assistant Prgm.
  241 Cowley Hall/1725 State St.
  La Crosse, WI 54601
  Tel: 608-785-6620 *Fax:* 608-785-6647
  E-mail: zellmer@mail.uwlax.edu

University of Wisconsin–Madison
  Physician Assistant Prgm.
  1300 University Ave./1050 MSC
  Madison, WI 53706
  Tel: 608-263-5620 *Fax:* 608-263-6434
  E-mail: jjnoack@facstaff. wisc.edu

Marquette University
  Physician Assistant Prgm.
  P.O. Box 1881
  Milwaukee, WI 53201-1881
  Tel: 414-288-5688 *Fax:* 414-288-7951

MEDICAL ASSISTANT TRAINING PROGRAMS

Alabama

George C. Wallace State Community
    College
    Medical Assistant Prgm.
    Napier Field Rd./Rte. 6 Box 62
    Dothan, AL 36303
    Tel: 334-983-3521 *Fax:* 334-983-3600

Wallace State College
    Medical Assistant Prgm.
    P.O. Box 2000
    Hanceville, AL 35077-2000
    Tel: 205-352-2090, ext. 235
    Fax: 205-352-8320

South Junior College
    Medical Assistant Prgm.
    122 Commerce St.
    Montgomery, AL 36104
    Tel: 334-263-1013 *Fax:* 334-262-7326

H. Councill Trenholm State Technical
    College
    Medical Assistant Prgm.
    1225 Air Base Blvd./ P.O. Box 9000
    Montgomery, AL 36108
    Tel: 334-832-9000 *Fax:* 334-832-9777

Alaska

University of Alaska Anchorage
    Medical Assistant Prgm.
    3211 Providence Dr.
    Anchorage, AK 99508
    Tel: 907-786-6932
    E-mail: AFRJW@uaa.alaska.edu

Arizona

The Bryman School
    Medical Assistant Prgm.
    4343 N. Sixteenth St.
    Phoenix, AZ 85016
    Tel: 602-274-4300 *Fax:* 602-230-9942

Arkansas

Arkansas Technical University
    Medical Assistant Prgm.
    Russellville, AR 72801
    Tel: 501-968-0328 *Fax:* 501-964-0504

California

ConCorde Career Institute
    Medical Assistant Prgm.
    1717 S. Brookhurst St.
    Anaheim, CA 92804
    Tel: 714-635-3450 *Fax:* 714-535-3168

Orange Coast College
    Medical Assistant Prgm.
    2701 Fairview Rd.
    Costa Mesa, CA 92628-5005
    Tel: 714-432-0202 *Fax:* 714-432-5534

De Anza College
    Medical Assistant Prgm.
    21250 Stevens Creek Blvd.
    Cupertino, CA 95014
    Tel: 408-864-8789 *Fax:* 408-864-5444

Silicon Valley College
    Medical Assistant Prgm.
    41350 Christy St.
    Fremont, CA 94538
    Tel: 510-623-9966 *Fax:* 510-623-9822

Chabot College
    Medical Assistant Prgm.
    25555 Hesperian Blvd.
    Hayward, CA 94545-5001
    Tel: 510-786-6901 *Fax:* 510-782-9315

Modesto Junior College
    Medical Assistant Prgm.
    435 College Ave.
    Modesto, CA 95350-9977
    Tel: 209-575-6377

Bryman College
    Medical Assistant Prgm.
    1120 W. La Veta/Ste. 100
    Orange, CA 92668
    Tel: 714-953-6500 *Fax:* 714-953-4163

Pasadena City College
    Medical Assistant Prgm.
    1570 E. Colorado Blvd.
    Pasadena, CA 91106
    Tel: 818-585-7431

National Education Center–Bryman
　　Campus
Medical Assistant Prgm.
3505 N. Hart Ave.
Rosemead, CA 91770
Tel: 818-573-5470 *Fax:* 818-280-4011

Cosumnes River College
Medical Assistant Prgm.
8401 Center Pkwy.
Sacramento, CA 95823
Tel: 916-688-7296 *Fax:* 916-688-7443

Western Career College
Medical Assistant Prgm.
8909 Folsom Blvd.
Sacramento, CA 95826
Tel: 916-361-1660 *Fax:* 916-361-6666

ConCorde Career Institute
Medical Assistant Prgm.
570 W. Fourth St.
San Bernardino, CA 92401
Tel: 909-884-8891 *Fax:* 909-384-1768

National Education Center–Skadron
　　Campus
Medical Assistant Prgm.
825 E. Hospitality Ln.
San Bernardino, CA 92408
Tel: 909-885-3893 *Fax:* 909-885-2396

San Diego Mesa College
Medical Assistant Prgm.
7250 Mesa College Dr.
San Diego, CA 92111
Tel: 619-627-2945 *Fax:* 619-627-2741
E-mail: talmukhj@intergate.
　　sdmes.cc.ca.us

City College of San Francisco
Medical Assistant Prgm.
1860 Hayes St.
San Francisco, CA 94117
Tel: 415-561-1826 *Fax:* 415-561-1861

National Education Center–Bryman
　　Campus
Medical Assistant Prgm.
731 Market St.
San Francisco, CA 94103
Tel: 415-777-2500 *Fax:* 415-495-3457

National Education Center–Bryman
　　Campus
Medical Assistant Prgm.
1245 Winchester Blvd.
San Jose, CA 95128
Tel: 408-246-4171 *Fax:* 408-557-9855

Sawyer College
Medical Assistant Prgm.
441 W. Trimble Rd.
San Jose, CA 95131
Tel: 408-954-8200 *Fax:* 408-944-0949

Western Career College of San
　　Leandro
Medical Assistant Prgm.
170 Bayfair Mall
San Leandro, CA 94578
Tel: 510-276-3888 *Fax:* 510-276-3653

Center of Employment Training
Medical Assistant Prgm.
120 W. Fifth St./Ste. 120
Santa Ana, CA 92701
Tel: 714-568-1755 *Fax:* 714-568-1331

Center of Employment Training
Medical Assistant Prgm.
509 W. Morrison Ave.
Santa Maria, CA 93454
Tel: 805-928-1737 *Fax:* 805-928-1203

Coastal Valley College
Medical Assistant Prgm.
731 S. Lincoln St.
Santa Maria, CA 93454
Tel: 805-925-1478 *Fax:* 805-925-4189

West Valley Community College
　　District
Medical Assistant Prgm.
14000 Fruitvale Ave.
Saratoga, CA 95070
Tel: 408-741-2498
E-mail: faraneh.javan@westvaley.edu

National Education Center–Bryman
　　Campus
Medical Assistant Prgm.
4212 W. Artesia Blvd.
Torrance, CA 90504
Tel: 310-542-6951 *Fax:* 310-542-3294

Colorado

T. H. Pickens Technical Center
Medical Assistant Prgm.
500 Airport Blvd.
Aurora, CO 80011
Tel: 303-344-4910 *Fax:* 303-326-1277

Front Range Community
College–Westminster
Medical Assistant Prgm.
6600 Arapahoe
Boulder, Co 80303
Tel: 303-447-5588 *Fax:* 303-447-5258

Blair College
Medical Assistant Prgm.
828 Wooten Rd.
Colorado Springs, CO 80915
Tel: 719-574-1082 *Fax:* 719-574-4493

Community College of Denver
Medical Assistant Prgm.
3532 Franklin St.
Denver, CO 80205
Tel: 303-293-8737 *Fax:* 303-292-4315

Westwood College of Technology
Medical Assistant Prgm.
Health Careers Div.
7350 N. Broadway
Denver, CO 80221
Tel: 303-650-5050

Emily Griffith Opportunity School
Medical Assistant Prgm.
1250 Welton St.
Denver, CO 80204
Tel: 303-575-4737 *Fax:* 303-575-4840

Parks College
Medical Assistant Prgm.
9065 Grant St.
Denver, CO 80229
Tel: 303-457-2757 *Fax:* 303-457-4030

Connecticut

Branford Hall Career Institute
Medical Assistant Prgm.
One Summit Pl.
Branford, CT 06405
Tel: 203-488-2525 *Fax:* 203-488-5233
E-mail: brandford@ micro-net.com

Quinebaug Valley Community–Tech
College
Medical Assistant Prgm.
742 Upper Maple St.
Danielson, CT 06239
Tel: 860-774-1160 *Fax:* 860-774-7768
E-mail: qr_markos_76
@apollo.columnet.edu

Data Institute Business School
Medical Assistant Prgm.
745 Burnside Ave.
East Hartford, CT 06108
Tel: 860-528-4111 *Fax:* 860-291-9550

Porter and Chester Institute–Enfield
Medical Assistant Prgm.
132 Weymouth Rd.
Enfield, CT 06082
Tel: 860-741-2561 *Fax:* 860-741-0234

Stone Academy
Medical Assistant Prgm.
1315 Dixwell Ave.
Hamden, CT 06514
Tel: 203-288-7474 *Fax:* 203-288-8869

Morse School of Business
Medical Assistant Prgm.
275 Asylum St.
Hartford, CT 06103
Tel: 860-522-2261

Ridley–Lowell Business and Technical
College
Medical Assistant Prgm.
470 Bank St.
New London, CT 06320
Tel: 860-443-7441 *Fax:* 860-442-3096

Porter and Chester Institute–Stratford
Medical Assistant Prgm.
670 Lordship Blvd.
Stratford, CT 06497
Tel: 203-375-4463 *Fax:* 203-375-5285

Porter and Chester
Institute–Watertown
Medical Assistant Prgm.
320 Sylvan Lake Rd.
Watertown, CT 06779
Tel: 203-274-9294 *Fax:* 203-274-3075

Fox Institute of Business
  Medical Assistant Prgm.
  99 South St.
  West Hartford, CT 06110-1922
  Tel: 860-947-2299 *Fax:* 860-947-2290
  E-mail: patrickfox@aol.com

Porter and Chester
    Institute–Wethersfield
  Medical Assistant Prgm.
  125 Silas Deane Hwy.
  Wethersfield, CT 06109
  Tel: 203-529-2519 *Fax:* 203-563-2595

Northwestern Connecticut Community
    College
  Medical Assistant Prgm.
  Park Place E.
  Winsted, CT 06098
  Tel: 860-738-6378 *Fax:* 860-738-6439
  E-mail: nw_berger

Florida

Keiser College of Technology
  Medical Assistant Prgm.
  1500 NW Forty-Ninth St.
  Daytona Beach, FL 33309
  Tel: 954-776-4456 *Fax:* 954-771-4894

Broward Community College
  Medical Assistant Prgm.
  3501 SW Davie Rd.
  Ft. Lauderdale, FL 33301
  Tel: 954-475-6906 *Fax:* 954-473-9037

International College of Ft. Myers
  Medical Assistant Prgm.
  8695 College Pkwy./Ste. 217
  Ft. Myers, FL 33919
  Tel: 941-482-0019 *Fax:* 941-482-1714

Orlando College–Melbourne Campus
  Medical Assistant Prgm.
  2401 N. Harbor City Blvd.
  Melbourne, FL 32935
  Tel: 407-253-2929 *Fax:* 407-255-2017

Haney Vocational Technical Center
  Medical Assistant Prgm.
  3016 Highway 77
  Panama City, FL 32405
  Tel: 904-747-5500 *Fax:* 904-747-5555

Pensacola Junior College
  Medical Assistant Prgm.
  Warrington Campus
  5555 W. Hwy. 98
  Pensacola, FL 32507
  Tel: 904-484-2223 *Fax:* 904-454-2365

North Technical Education Center
  Medical Assistant Prgm.
  7071 Garden Rd.
  Riviera Beach, FL 33404
  Tel: 561-881-4614 *Fax:* 561-881-4669

Sarasota County Technical Institute
  Medical Assistant Prgm.
  4748 Beneva Rd.
  Sarasota, FL 34233
  Tel: 941-924-1365 *Fax:* 941-361-6886

Pinellas Technical Educational
    Center–St. Petersburg
  Medical Assistant Prgm.
  901 Thirty-Fourth St. S
  St. Petersburg, FL 33711
  Tel: 813-893-2500 *Fax:* 813-893-2776

Lively Technical Center
  Medical Assistant Prgm.
  500 N. Appleyard Dr.
  Tallahassee, FL 32304
  Tel: 904-487-7452 *Fax:* 904-922-3880

David G. Erwin Technical Center
  Medical Assistant Prgm.
  2010 E. Hillsborough Ave.
  Tampa, FL 33610-8299
  Tel: 813-231-1800 *Fax:* 813-231-1820

New England Institute of Technology
    at Palm Beach
  Medical Assistant Prgm.
  1126 Fifty-Third Ct.
  West Palm Beach, FL 33407
  Tel: 561-842-8324 *Fax:* 561-842-9503

South College
  Medical Assistant Prgm.
  1760 N. Congress Ave.
  West Palm Beach, FL 33409
  Tel: 561-697-9200

Winter Park Tech
  Medical Assistant Prgm.
  901 Webster Ave.
  Winter Park, FL 32789
  Tel: 407-647-6366 *Fax:* 407-647-6366
  E-mail: mattheb@ocps.k12.fl.us

Georgia

Atlanta Area Technical School
Medical Assistant Prgm.
1560 Stewart Ave. SW
Atlanta, GA 30310
Tel: 404-756-3779 *Fax:* 404-756-0932

Augusta Technical Institute
Medical Assistant Prgm.
3116 Deans Bridge Rd.
Augusta, GA 30906
Tel: 706-771-4189 *Fax:* 706-771-4181
E-mail: Inagle@augusta.tec. ga.us

Columbus Technical Institute
Medical Assistant Prgm.
928 Forty-Fifth St.
Columbus, GA 31904-6572
Tel: 706-649-1499 *Fax:* 706-649-1937

Heart of Georgia Technical Institute
Medical Assistant Prgm.
560 Pinehill Rd.
Dublin, GA 31021
Tel: 912-274-7885 *Fax:* 912-275-6642

Savannah Technical Institute
Medical Assistant Prgm.
5717 White Bluff Rd.
Savannah, GA 31405-5594
Tel: 912-351-4562 *Fax:* 912-352-4362

South College
Medical Assistant Prgm.
709 Mall Blvd.
Savannah, GA 31406
Tel: 912-691-6000 *Fax:* 912-691-6070
E-mail: southcollege@sava.
  gulfnet.com

Medix School
Medical Assistant Prgm.
2108 Cobb Pkwy.
Smyrna, GA 30080
Tel: 770-980-0002 *Fax:* 770-980-0811

Swainsboro Technical Institute
Medical Assistant Prgm.
346 Kite Rd.
Swainsboro, GA 30401
Tel: 912-237-6465, ext. 32
Fax: 912-237-4043
E-mail: gfulcher@admin1.
  swainsboro.tec.ga.us

Thomas Technical Institute
Medical Assistant Prgm.
15689 US Hwy. 19 North
Thomasville, GA 31792
Tel: 912-225-5081 *Fax:* 912-225-5289

Valdosta Technical Institute
Medical Assistant Prgm.
4089 Valtec Rd./P.O. Box 928
Valdosta, GA 31603-0928
Tel: 912-333-2100 *Fax:* 912-333-2129

Hawaii

Kapiolani Community College
Medical Assistant Prgm.
4303 Diamond Head Rd.
Honolulu, HI 96816
Tel: 808-734-9349 *Fax:* 808-734-9126
E-mail: jyoung@leahi.kcc.hawaii.edu

Idaho

College of Southern Idaho
Medical Assistant Prgm.
P.O. Box 1238
Twin Falls, ID 83303-1238
Tel: 208-733-9554 *Fax:* 208-736-4743
E-mail: pglenn@aspent.csi.cc.id.us

Illinois

Belleville Area College
Medical Assistant Prgm.
2500 Carlyle Rd.
Belleville, IL 62221
Tel: 618-235-2700 *Fax:* 618-235-1578

Northwestern Business College
Medical Assistant Prgm.
4829 N. Lipps Ave.
Chicago, IL 60630
Tel: 773-481-3756 *Fax:* 773-481-2995

Robert Morris College
Medical Assistant Prgm.
180 N. LaSalle St.
Chicago, IL 60601
Tel: 312-836-4888

Northwestern Business College
Medical Assistant Prgm.
Southwest Campus
8020 W. Eighty-Seventh St.
Hickory Hills, IL 60457
Tel: 773-481-3756 *Fax:* 773-481-2995

Robert Morris College
Medical Assistant Prgm.
43 N. Orland Square Dr.
Orland Park, IL 60462
Tel: 708-349-5122 *Fax:* 708-349-5119

William Rainey Harper College
Medical Assistant Prgm.
1200 W. Algonquin Rd.
Palatine, IL 60067
Tel: 847-925-6444 *Fax:* 847-925-6047

Midstate College
Medical Assistant Prgm.
411 W. Northmoor Rd.
Peoria, IL 61614
Tel: 309-673-6365 *Fax:* 309-673-5814

Rockford Business College
Medical Assistant Prgm.
730 N. Church
Rockford, IL 61103
Tel: 815-965-8616 *Fax:* 815-965-0360

Robert Morris College
Medical Assistant Prgm.
3101 Montvale Dr.
Springfield, IL 62704
Tel: 217-793-2500 *Fax:* 217-793-4210

Indiana

Ivy Tech State College–Columbus
Medical Assistant Prgm.
4475 Central Ave.
Columbus, IN 47203
Tel: 812-372-9925, ext. 135
Fax: 812-372-0311
E-mail: mryser@ivy.tec.in.us

Indiana Business College–Evansville
Medical Assistant Prgm.
4601 Theater Dr.
Evansville, IN 47715
Tel: 812-476-6000 *Fax:* 812-471-8576

Ivy Tech State College SW–Evansville
Medical Assistant Prgm.
3501 First Ave.
Evansville, IN 47710
Tel: 812-429-1381 *Fax:* 812-429-1483

International Business College–Ft.
Wayne
Medical Assistant Prgm.
3811 Old Illinois Rd.
Ft Wayne, IN 46804-1298
Tel: 219-432-8702 *Fax:* 219-436-1896

Ivy Tech State College NE–Ft. Wayne
Medical Assistant Prgm.
3800 N. Anthony Blvd.
Ft. Wayne, IN 46805
Tel: 219-480-4273 *Fax:* 219-480-4149

Michiana College
Medical Assistant Prgm.
4807 Illinois Rd.
Ft. Wayne, IN 46804
Tel: 219-237-0774 *Fax:* 219-237-3585

Indiana Business College–Indianapolis
Medical Assistant Prgm.
5460 Victory Dr./Ste. 100
Indianapolis, IN 46204
Tel: 317-783-5100 *Fax:* 317-783-4898

International Business
College–Indianapolis
Medical Assistant Prgm.
7205 Shadeland Station
Indianapolis, IN 46256
Tel: 317-841-6400 *Fax:* 317-841-6419

Ivy Tech State College–Indianapolis
Central Indiana Region
Medical Assistant Prgm.
One W. Twenty-Sixth St./P.O. Box
1763
Indianapolis, IN 46206-1763
Tel: 317-921-4450 *Fax:* 317-921-4511
E-mail: lreed@ivy.tec.in.us

Professional Careers Institute
Medical Assistant Prgm.
2611 Waterfront Pkwy. E. Dr.
Indianapolis, IN 46214
Tel: 317-299-6001 *Fax:* 317-298-6842

Ivy Tech State College–Kokomo
Medical Assistant Prgm.
1815 E. Morgan St.
Kokomo, IN 46901
Tel: 765-459-0561, ext. 377
Fax: 765-454-5111

Ivy Tech State College–Lafayette
Medical Assistant Prgm.
3101 S. Creasy Ln./ P.O. Box 6299
Lafayette, IN 47903
Tel: 317-772-9206 *Fax:* 317-772-9214

Ivy Tech State College–Madison
Medical Assistant Prgm.
Health & Human Services Div.
590 IVY Tech Dr.
Madison, IN 47250
Tel: 812-265-2580

Ivy Tech State College EC–Muncie
Medical Assistant Prgm.
4301 Cowan Rd.
Muncie, IN 47307
Tel: 765-289-2291 *Fax:* 765-289-2291

Ivy Tech State College–Richmond
Medical Assistant Prgm.
2325 Chester Blvd.
Richmond, IN 47374
Tel: 765-966-2656, ext. 372
Fax: 765-962-8741
E-mail: ibond@ivytech.in.us

Ivy Tech State College SC–Sellersburg
Medical Assistant Prgm.
8204 Hwy. 311
Sellersburg, IN 47172
Tel: 812-246-3301 *Fax:* 812-246-9905
E-mail: drawles@ivy.tec.in.us

Ivy Tech State College NC–South
Bend
Medical Assistant Prgm.
1534 W. Sample St.
South Bend, IN 46619
Tel: 219-289-7001 *Fax:* 219-236-7172
E-mail: mgarrels@ivy.tec. in.us

Michiana College
Medical Assistant Prgm.
1030 E. Jefferson Blvd.
South Bend, IN 46617
Tel: 219-436-2738 *Fax:* 219-436-2958

Ivy Tech State College– Terre Haute
Medical Assistant Prgm.
7999 US Hwy. 41 S.
Terre Haute, IN 47802-4898
Tel: 812-299-1121 *Fax:* 812-299-5723
E-mail: jroloff@ivy.tec.in.us

Ivy Tech State College–Valparaiso
Medical Assistant Prgm.
2401 Valley Dr.
Valparaiso, IN 46383
Tel: 219-464-8514 *Fax:* 219-464-9751

Iowa

Des Moines Area Community College
Medical Assistant Prgm.
2006 Ankeny Blvd.
Ankeny, IA 50021
Tel: 515-964-6457 *Fax:* 515-964-6440

Kirkwood Community College
Medical Assistant Prgm.
6301 Kirkwood Blvd. SW/P.O. Box
2068
Cedar Rapids, IA 52406-9973
Tel: 319-398-5564 *Fax:* 319-398-1293

Iowa Western Community College
Medical Assistant Prgm.
2700 College Rd./ P.O. Box 4-C
Council Bluffs, IA 51502-3004
Tel: 712-325-3348 *Fax:* 712-325-3717

American Institute of Commerce
Medical Assistant Prgm.
1801 E. Kimberly Rd.
Davenport, IA 52807
Tel: 319-355-3500

Hamilton College
Medical Assistant Prgm.
2300 Euclid Ave.
Des Moines, IA 50310
Tel: 515-279-0253 *Fax:* 515-279-2054

Iowa Central Community College
Medical Assistant Prgm.
330 Ave. M
Ft. Dodge, IA 50501
Tel: 515-576-7201 *Fax:* 515-576-7206
E-mail: kolesar@duke.iccc.cc.ia.us

Iowa Lakes Community College
Medical Assistant Prgm.
217 W. Fifth St.
Spencer, IA 51301
Tel: 712-262-8428

Southeastern Community College
Medical Assistant Prgm.
1015 S. Gear Ave./Drawer F
West Burlington, IA 52655
Tel: 319-752-2731 *Fax:* 319-752-4957

Kansas

Wichita Area Technical College
Medical Assistant Prgm.
324 N. Emporia
Wichita, KS 67202
Tel: 316-833-4370

Kentucky

Kentucky College of
Business–Danville
Medical Assistant Prgm.
115 E. Lexington Ave.
Danville, KY 40422
Tel: 606-236-6991 *Fax:* 606-236-1063

Kentucky College of Business–
Florence
Medical Assistant Prgm.
7627 Ewing Blvd.
Florence, KY 41042
Tel: 606-525-6510 *Fax:* 606-525-2815

Fugazzi College
Medical Assistant Prgm.
407 Marquis Ave.
Lexington, KY 40502
Tel: 606-266-0401 *Fax:* 606-268-2118

Kentucky Tech Central Campus
Medical Assistant Prgm.
308 Vo-Tech Rd.
Lexington, KY 40511
Tel: 606-246-2400, ext. 254
Fax: 606-246-2417

Kentucky College of
Business–Louisville
Medical Assistant Prgm.
3950 Dixie Hwy.
Louisville, KY 40216-4147
Tel: 502-447-7634 *Fax:* 502-447-7665

Kentucky Tech/Jefferson State Campus
Medical Assistant Prgm.
800 W. Chestnut St.
Louisville, KY 40203
Tel: 502-595-4275 *Fax:* 502-595-2387

Spencerian College
Medical Assistant Prgm.
4627 Dixie Hwy.
Louisville, KY 40216
Tel: 502-447-1000 *Fax:* 502-447-4574

West Kentucky Tech
Medical Assistant Prgm.
Blandville Rd./P.O. Box 7408
Paducah, KY 42002-7408
Tel: 502-554-4991 *Fax:* 502-554-2695

Kentucky College of
Business–Pikeville
Medical Assistant Prgm.
198 S. Mayo Trail
Pikeville, KY 41501
Tel: 606-437-5477 *Fax:* 606-437-4952

Eastern Kentucky University
Medical Assistant Prgm.
Dizney 225
Richmond, KY 40475-3135
Tel: 606-622-1028 *Fax:* 606-622-1140
E-mail: masrenfr@asc.eku.edu

Kentucky College of
Business–Richmond
Medical Assistant Prgm.
139 Killarney Ln.
Richmond, KY 40475
Tel: 606-623-8956 *Fax:* 606-624-5544

Maine

Beal College
Medical Assistant Prgm.
629 Main St.
Bangor, ME 04401
Tel: 207-947-4591 *Fax:* 207-947-0208

Husson College
Medical Assistant Prgm.
One College Circle
Bangor, ME 04401
Tel: 207-941-7169 *Fax:* 207-941-7988
E-mail: perry@husson.husson.edu

Maryland

Medix School
Medical Assistant Prgm.
1017 York Rd.
Towson, MD 21204
Tel: 410-337-5155 *Fax:* 410-337-5104

Massachusetts

Porter and Chester Institute–Chicopee
Medical Assistant Prgm.
134 Dulong Circle
Chicopee, MA 01022
Tel: 413-593-3339, ext. 128
Fax: 413-593-6439

Northern Essex Community College
Medical Assistant Prgm.
100 Elliott Way
Haverhill, MA 01830
Tel: 508-374-3884 *Fax:* 508-374-3729

Aquinas College at Milton
Medical Assistant Prgm.
303 Adams St.
Milton, MA 02186
Tel: 617-696-3100 *Fax:* 617-696-8706

Southeastern Technical Institute
Medical Assistant Prgm.
250 Foundry St.
S. Easton, MA 02375
Tel: 508-238-1860 *Fax:* 508-238-7266

Springfield Technical Community
College
Medical Assistant Prgm.
One Amory Square
P.O. Box 9000
Springfield, MA 01105
Tel: 413-781-7822 *Fax:* 413-781-5805

The Salter School
Medical Assistant Prgm.
155 Ararat St.
Worcester, MA 01606-3450
Tel: 508-853-1074 *Fax:* 508-853-1083

Worcester Technical Institute
Medical Assistant Prgm.
251 Belmont St.
Worcester, MA 01605
Tel: 508-799-1945 *Fax:* 508-799-1932

Michigan

Alpena Community College
Medical Assistant Prgm.
666 Johnson St.
Alpena, MI 49707
Tel: 517-356-9021, ext. 226
Fax: 517-356-0980

Baker College of Auburn Hills
Medical Assistant Prgm.
1500 University Dr.
Auburn Hills, MI 48326
Tel: 810-340-0600, ext. 131
Fax: 810-340-0608

Great Lakes College–Bay City
Medical Assistant Prgm.
3930 Traxler Court
Bay City, MI 48706
Tel: 517-673-5857 *Fax:* 517-673-7543

Great Lakes College–Caro
Medical Assistant Prgm.
1231 Cleaver Rd.
Caro, MI 48723
Tel: 517-673-5857 *Fax:* 517-673-7543

Baker College of Mt. Clemens
Medical Assistant Prgm.
34950 Little Mack Ave.
Clinton Township, MI 48035
Tel: 810-791-6610 *Fax:* 810-791-6611

Macomb Community College
Medical Assistant Prgm.
Business Health & Human Services
44575 Garfield Rd.
Clinton Township, MI 48038-1139
Tel: 810-286-2097 *Fax:* 810-286-2098

Henry Ford Community College
Medical Assistant Prgm.
22586 Ann Arbor Trail
Dearborn Heights, MI 48127
Tel: 313-730-5974 *Fax:* 313-730-5965

Baker College
Medical Assistant Prgm.
G 1050 W. Bristol Rd.
Flint, MI 48507
Tel: 810-766-4133 *Fax:* 810-766-4049
E-mail: Benedi_m@acadfl.baker.edu

Davenport College
Medical Assistant Prgm.
415 E. Fulton St.
Grand Rapids, MI 49503
Tel: 616-451-3511 *Fax:* 616-732-1142

Jackson Community College
Medical Assistant Prgm.
2111 Emmons Rd.
Jackson, MI 48201
Tel: 517-796-8557 *Fax:* 517-796-8311
E-mail: Jean_Dennerll@
Jackson.cc.mi.us

Kalamazoo Valley Community College
Medical Assistant Prgm.
P.O. Box 4070
6767 West O Ave.
Kalamazoo, MI 49003
Tel: 616-372-5324 *Fax:* 616-372-5458

Great Lakes College–Midland
Medical Assistant Prgm.
3555 E. Patrick Rd.
Midland, MI 48642
Tel: 517-673-5857 *Fax:* 517-673-7543

Baker College of Muskegon
Medical Assistant Prgm.
123 Apple Ave.
Muskegon, MI 49442
Tel: 616-726-4904 *Fax:* 616-728-1417
E-mail: kenny_t@muskegon.
    baker.edu

Baker College of Owosso
Medical Assistant Prgm.
1020 S. Washington St.
Owosso, MI 48867
Tel: 517-723-5251 *Fax:* 517-723-3355

Great Lakes College–Saginaw
Medical Assistant Prgm.
310 S. Washington Ave.
Saginaw, MI 48607
Tel: 517-673-5857 *Fax:* 517-673-7543

Carnegie Institute
Medical Assistant Prgm.
550 Stephenson Hwy./Ste. 100
Troy, MI 48083
Tel: 248-589-1078 *Fax:* 248-589-1631
E-mail: carnegie47@aol.com

Oakland Community
    College–Waterford
Medical Assistant Prgm.
7350 Cooley Lake Rd.
Waterford, MI 48327
Tel: 248-360-3094 *Fax:* 248-360-3203

Minnesota

Anoka–Hennepin Technical College
Medical Assistant Prgm.
1355 W. Hwy. 10
Anoka, MN 55303
Tel: 612-427-1880 *Fax:* 612-576-4715

Medical Institute of Minnesota
Medical Assistant Prgm.
5503 Green Valley Dr.
Bloomington, MN 55437
Tel: 612-844-0064 *Fax:* 612-844-0671

Duluth Business University/MN
    School of Business
Medical Assistant Prgm.
412 W. Superior St.
Duluth, MN 55802
Tel: 218-722-3361 *Fax:* 218-722-8376

Northwest Technical College–East
    Grand Forks
Medical Assistant Prgm.
2022 Central Ave. NE
East Grand Forks, MN 56721
Tel: 218-773-3441
E-mail: mcmahon@mail.ntc.
    mnscu.edu

Lakeland Medical Dental Academy
Medical Assistant Prgm.
1402 W. Lake St.
Minneapolis, MN 55408
Tel: 612-827-5656

Minnesota School of
    Business–Richfield
Medical Assistant Prgm.
1401 W. Seventy-Sixth St./Ste. 500
Richfield, MN 55423
Tel: 612-798-3726 *Fax:* 612-861-5548

Rochester Community and Technical
    College
Medical Assistant Prgm.
851 Thirtieth Ave. SE
Rochester, MN 55904-4999
Tel: 507-285-7117 *Fax:* 507-285-7496
E-mail: mreif@ucrpo.roch. edu

Dakota County Technical College
Medical Assistant Prgm.
1300 E. 145th St.
Rosemount, MN 55068-2999
Tel: 612-423-8355, ext. 355
Fax: 612-423-8775
E-mail: Dtemp@dak.tec. mn.us

Minneapolis Business College
Medical Assistant Prgm.
1711 W. County Rd. B
Roseville, MN 55113
Tel: 612-636-7406

Globe College of Business
  Medical Assistant Prgm.
  175 Fifth St. E./Ste. 201
  Galtier Plaza Box 60
  St. Paul, MN 55101-2901
  Tel: 612-798-3726 *Fax:* 612-861-5548

Century Community and Technical
    College
  Medical Assistant Prgm.
  3300 Century Ave. N
  White Bear Lake, MN 55110
  Tel: 612-773-1731

Ridgewater College–Willmar Campus
  Medical Assistant Prgm.
  2101 Fifteenth Ave. NW/P.O. Box
    1097
  Willmar, MN 56201
  Tel: 320-231-2947 *Fax:* 320-231-7677

Mississippi

Northeast Mississippi Community
    College
  Medical Assistant Prgm.
  Cunningham Blvd.
  Booneville, MS 38829
  Tel: 601-720-7393 *Fax:* 601-728-1165

Hinds Community College District
  Medical Assistant Prgm.
  3805 Hwy. 80 E
  Pearl, MS 39208
  Tel: 601-932-5582 *Fax:* 601-936-5569

Missouri

Springfield College
  Medical Assistant Prgm.
  1010 W. Sunshine St.
  Springfield, MO 65807-2446
  Tel: 417-864-7220 *Fax:* 417-864-5697

Montana

Montana State University College of
    Technology
  Medical Assistant Prgm.
  2100 Sixteenth Ave. S
  Great Falls, MT 59405
  Tel: 406-771-4383 *Fax:* 406-771-4317

Nebraska

Grand Island College
  Medical Assistant Prgm.
  410 W. Second St.
  Grand Island, NE 68801
  Tel: 308-382-8044 *Fax:* 308-382-5072

Central Community College
  Medical Assistant Prgm.
  Hastings Campus/ P.O. Box 1024
  Hastings, NE 68902-1024
  Tel: 402-461-2473 *Fax:* 402-461-2473
  E-mail: wiehmea@
    ccadm.gi.cccneb.edu

Southeast Community College
  Medical Assistant Prgm.
  8800 O St.
  Lincoln, NE 68520
  Tel: 402-437-2756

Omaha College of Health Careers
  Medical Assistant Prgm.
  10845 Harney St.
  Omaha, NE 68154-2655
  Tel: 402-333-1400 *Fax:* 402-333-4598

New Hampshire

New Hampshire Community
    Technical College
  Medical Assistant Prgm.
  One College Dr.
  Claremont, NH 03743
  Tel: 603-542-7744 *Fax:* 603-543-1844
  E-mail: a_halste@tec.nh.us

Northeast Career Schools
  Medical Assistant Prgm.
  25 Lowell St.
  Manchester, NH 03101
  Tel: 603-669-1151, ext. 533
  Fax: 603-622-2866

New Jersey

Hudson County Community College
  Medical Assistant Prgm.
  2039 Kennedy Blvd./Science 330
  Jersey City, NJ 07305
  Tel: 201-200-3320 *Fax:* 201-200-2298
  E-mail: JABender@AOL

Bergen Community College
  Medical Assistant Prgm.
  400 Paramus Rd.
  Paramus, NJ 07652
  Tel: 201-447-7944 *Fax:* 201-612-8225

Dover Business College– Paramus
  Medical Assistant Prgm.
  81 E. Rte. 4 W
  Paramus, NJ 07652
  Tel: 201-843-8500 *Fax:* 201-843-3896

Dover Business College–Parsippany
  Medical Assistant Prgm.
  1719 Rte. 10 E
  Parsippany, NJ 07054
  Tel: 973-285-8400 *Fax:* 973-285-0364

Technical Institute of Camden County
  Medical Assistant Prgm.
  Cross Keys Rd./P.O. Box 566
  Sicklerville, NJ 08081
  Tel: 609-767-7000 *Fax:* 609-767-6625

Berdan Institute
  Medical Assistant Prgm.
  265 Rte. 46 W
  Totowa, NJ 07512
  Tel: 201-256-3444 *Fax:* 201-256-0816

Warren County Community College
  Medical Assistant Prgm.
  475 Rte. 57 W
  Washington, NJ 07882
  Tel: 908-835-2430 *Fax:* 908-689-8032

New Mexico

Franklin College
  Medical Assistant Prgm.
  2400 Louisiana NE
  Ste. 200 AFC-3
  Albuquerque, NM 87110
  Tel: 505-883-4800 *Fax:* 505-881-3226

New York

Bryant & Stratton Business Institute
  Medical Assistant Prgm.
  1259 Central Ave.
  Albany, NY 12205
  Tel: 518-437-1802 *Fax:* 518-437-1048

Broome Community College
  Medical Assistant Prgm.
  Decker Bldg./P.O. Box 1017
  Binghamton, NY 13902
  Tel: 607-778-5161 *Fax:* 607-778-5345

Ridley–Lowell Business & Technical
    Institute
  Medical Assistant Prgm.
  116 Front St.
  Binghamton, NY 13905
  Tel: 607-724-2941 *Fax:* 607-724-0799

Suffolk Community College
  Medical Assistant Prgm.
  Crooked Hill Rd.
  Brentwood, NY 11717
  Tel: 516-851-6340 *Fax:* 516-851-6339

Bryant & Stratton Business Institute
  Medical Assistant Prgm.
  1028 Main St.
  Buffalo, NY 14202
  Tel: 716-884-9120

Trocaire College
  Medical Assistant Prgm.
  110 Red Jacket Pkwy.
  Buffalo, NY 14220
  Tel: 716-826-1200 *Fax:* 716-826-0059

Wood–Tobe Coburn School
  Medical Assistant Prgm.
  8 E. Fortieth St.
  New York, NY 10016
  Tel: 212-686-9040 *Fax:* 212-686-9171

Bryant & Stratton Business Institute
  Medical Assistant Prgm.
  82 St. Paul St.
  Rochester, NY 14604
  Tel: 716-325-6010 *Fax:* 716-325-6805

Bryant & Stratton Business Institute
  Medical Assistant Prgm.
  Henrietta Campus/1225 Jefferson Rd.
  Rochester, NY 14623-3136
  Tel: 716-292-5627 *Fax:* 716-292-6015

Bryant & Stratton Business Institute
  Medical Assistant Prgm.
  953 James St.
  Syracuse, NY 13202
  Tel: 315-472-6603 *Fax:* 315-474-4383

Central City Business Institute
  Medical Assistant Prgm.
  224 Harrison St.
  Syracuse, NY 13202
  Tel: 315-472-6233 *Fax:* 315-472-6201

Erie Community College–City
  Campus
  Medical Assistant Prgm.
  North Campus/6205 Main St.
  Williamsville, NY 14221-7095
  Tel: 716-851-1553 *Fax:* 716-851-1429

North Carolina

Cecils College
  Medical Assistant Prgm.
  P.O. Box 6407
  Asheville, NC 28816
  Tel: 704-252-2486 *Fax:* 704-252-8558

Central Piedmont Community College
  Medical Assistant Prgm.
  P.O. Box 35009
  Charlotte, NC 28235
  Tel: 704-330-6928 *Fax:* 704-330-5930
  E-mail: janice_mayhew@
    cprc.cc.nc.us

King's College
  Medical Assistant Prgm.
  322 Lamar Ave.
  Charlotte, NC 28204
  Tel: 704-372-0266 *Fax:* 704-348-2029

Haywood Community College
  Medical Assistant Prgm.
  Freelander Dr.
  Clyde, NC 28721-9454
  Tel: 704-627-4533 *Fax:* 704-627-4525

Gaston College
  Medical Assistant Prgm.
  201 Hwy. 321 S
  Dallas, NC 28034-1499
  Tel: 704-922-6377 *Fax:* 704-922-6484

Pitt Community College
  Medical Assistant Prgm.
  P.O. Drawer 7007/Hwy. 11 S
  Greenville, NC 27835-7007
  Tel: 919-355-4284 *Fax:* 919-321-4451
  E-mail: mhemby@pcc.pitt.cc.nc.us

Guilford Technical Community
  College
  Medical Assistant Prgm.
  P.O. Box 309
  Jamestown, NC 27282
  Tel: 910-334-4822 *Fax:* 910-454-2510

James Sprunt Community College
  Medical Assistant Prgm.
  JSCC P.O. Box 398/ Hwy. 11 S
  Kenansville, NC 28349
  Tel: 910-296-2565 *Fax:* 910-296-1636

Lenoir Community College
  Medical Assistant Prgm.
  P.O. Box 188/ Hwy. 70 E Bypass
  Kinston, NC 28502-0188
  Tel: 919-527-6223, ext. 502
  Fax: 919-527-1199
  E-mail: isj502@wpmail.
    lenoir.cc.nc.us

Mitchell Community College
  Medical Assistant Prgm.
  219 N. Academy St.
  Mooresville, NC 28115
  Tel: 704-663-1923 *Fax:* 704-663-5239

Carteret Community College
  Medical Assistant Prgm.
  3505 Arendell St.
  Morehead City, NC 28557
  Tel: 919-247-3097, ext. 168
  Fax: 919-247-2514

Western Piedmont Community College
  Medical Assistant Prgm.
  1001 Burkemont Ave.
  Morganton, NC 28655
  Tel: 704-438-6129 *Fax:* 704-438-6015

Central Carolina Community
  College–Chatham
  Medical Assistant Prgm.
  Rte. 6 Box 4476
  Lillington, NC 27546
  Tel: 919-542-6495 *Fax:* 919-542-6798

Central Carolina Community
  College–Harnett
  Medical Assistant Prgm.
  764 West St.
  Pittsboro, NC 27312
  Tel: 919-542-6495 *Fax:* 919-542-6798

Anson Community College
  Medical Assistant Prgm.
  P.O. Box 126
  Polkton, NC 28135
  Tel: 704-272-7635 *Fax:* 704-272-8904

Wake Technical Community College
Medical Assistant Prgm.
9101 Fayetteville Rd.
Raleigh, NC 27603-5676
Tel: 919-231-4500 *Fax:* 919-250-4329

Miller–Motte Business College
Medical Assistant Prgm.
606 S. College Rd.
Wilmington, NC 28403
Tel: 910-392-4660 *Fax:* 910-799-6224

Ohio

Southern Ohio College–NE
Medical Assistant Prgm.
2791 Mogadore Rd.
Akron, OH 44312
Tel: 330-733-8766 *Fax:* 330-733-5853

University of Akron
Medical Assistant Prgm.
Akron, OH 44325-3702
Tel: 330-972-6515 *Fax:* 330-972-6952

Ashland County–West Holmes Career
  Center
Medical Assistant Prgm.
1783 State Rte. 60
Ashland, OH 44805
Tel: 419-289-3313 *Fax:* 419-289-3729

Stark State College of Technology
Medical Assistant Prgm.
6200 Frank Ave. NW
Canton, OH 44720
Tel: 330-494-6170 *Fax:* 330-966-6586

Fairfield Career Center (EVSD)
Medical Assistant Prgm.
4000 Columbus-Lancaster Rd.
Carroll, OH 43112
Tel: 614-756-9245 *Fax:* 614-837-9447

Cincinnati State Technical and
  Community College
Medical Assistant Prgm.
3520 Central Pkwy.
Cincinnati, OH 45223
Tel: 513-569-1676 *Fax:* 513-569-1659
E-mail: owatts@cinstate.cc.oh

Southern Ohio College–Woodlawn
Medical Assistant Prgm.
1011 Glendale-Milford Rd.
Cincinnati, OH 45215-1107
Tel: 513-771-2424 *Fax:* 513-771-3413

Cuyahoga Community College
Medical Assistant Prgm.
Metro Campus
700 Carnegie Ave.
Cleveland, OH 44115
Tel: 216-987-4438 *Fax:* 216-987-4438

MTI Business College
Medical Assistant Prgm.
1140 Euclid Ave./2nd Flr.
Cleveland, OH 44115-1603
Tel: 216-621-8228 *Fax:* 216-621-6488

Bradford School
Medical Assistant Prgm.
6170 Busch Blvd.
Columbus, OH 43229
Tel: 614-846-9410 *Fax:* 614-846-9656

Akron Medical–Dental Institute
Medical Assistant Prgm.
1625 Portage Trail
Cuyahoga Falls, OH 44223-2122
Tel: 330-928-3400 *Fax:* 330-928-1906

Miami–Jacobs College
Medical Assistant Prgm.
400 E. Second St./ P.O. Box 1433
Dayton, OH 45401
Tel: 513-461-5174

Ohio Institute of Photography and
  Technology
Medical Assistant Prgm.
Division of Allied Health
2029 Edgefield Rd.
Dayton, OH 45439
Tel: 513-294-6155 *Fax:* 513-294-2259

Sinclair Community College
Medical Assistant Prgm.
444 W. Third St.
Dayton, OH 45402
Tel: 513-449-5163 *Fax:* 513-226-7960

Ohio Valley Business College
Medical Assistant Prgm.
500 Maryland St./ P.O. Box 7000
East Liverpool, OH 43920
Tel: 330-330-1070 *Fax:* 330-385-4606

Southern State Community College
Medical Assistant Prgm.
200 Hobart Dr.
Hillsboro, OH 45133
Tel: 937-393-3431 *Fax:* 937-393-9370

Medina County Career Center
Medical Assistant Prgm.
1101 W. Liberty St.
Medina, OH 44256-9969
Tel: 216-725-8461

EHOVE Career Center
Medical Assistant Prgm.
316 W. Mason Rd.
Milan, OH 44846
Tel: 419-499-4663, ext. 279
Fax: 419-499-4076

Knox County Career Center
Medical Assistant Prgm.
306 Martinsburg Rd.
Mt. Vernon, OH 43050
Tel: 614-397-5820 *Fax:* 614-397-7040

Hocking Technical College
Medical Assistant Prgm.
3301 Hocking Pkwy.
Nelsonville, OH 45764-9704
Tel: 614-753-3591 *Fax:* 614-753-5105
E-mail: west_k@nelie.
  hocking.cc.oh.us

Bryant & Stratton College
Medical Assistant Prgm.
12955 Snow Rd.
Parma, OH 44130
Tel: 216-265-3151 *Fax:* 216-265-0325

Bryant & Stratton Business Institute
Medical Assistant Prgm.
691 Richmond Rd.
Richmond Heights, OH 44143
Tel: 216-461-3151 *Fax:* 216-461-2827

Belmont Technical College
Medical Assistant Prgm.
120 Fox-Shannon Place
St. Clairsville, OH 43950
Tel: 614-695-9500 *Fax:* 614-695-2247

Jefferson Community College
Medical Assistant Prgm.
4000 Sunset Blvd.
Steubenville, OH 43952
Tel: 614-264-5591

Davis Junior College of Business
Medical Assistant Prgm.
4747 Monroe St.
Toledo, OH 43623
Tel: 419-473-2700

University of Toledo
Medical Assistant Prgm.
Community & Technical College
2801 W. Bancroft St.
Toledo, OH 43606
Tel: 419-530-3149 *Fax:* 419-530-3096

Youngstown State University
Medical Assistant Prgm.
Department of Health Professions
One University Plaza
Youngstown, OH 44555
Tel: 330-742-1760 *Fax:* 330-742-2309

Muskingum Area Technical College
Medical Assistant Prgm.
1555 Newark Rd.
Zanesville, OH 43701
Tel: 614-454-2501 *Fax:* 614-454-0035

Oklahoma

Canadian Valley Area Vocational
  Technical School
Medical Assistant Prgm.
1401 Michigan Ave.
Chickasha, OK 73018
Tel: 405-224-7220 *Fax:* 405-222-3839

Tulsa Community College
Medical Assistant Prgm.
909 S. Boston Ave.
Tulsa, OK 74119
Tel: 918-595-7006

Oregon

Lane Community College
Medical Assistant Prgm.
400 E. Thirtieth Ave.
Eugene, OR 97405
Tel: 541-747-4501, ext. 2632
Fax: 541-744-4151

Mt. Hood Community College
Medical Assistant Prgm.
26000 SE Stark St.
Gresham, OR 97030
Tel: 503-667-7136 *Fax:* 503-667-7618
E-mail: bouldens@mhcc.cc. or.us

Clackamas Community College
Medical Assistant Prgm.
19600 S. Mololla Ave.
Oregon City, OR 97045
Tel: 503-657-6958 *Fax:* 503-655-5153

ConCorde Career Institute
  Medical Assistant Prgm.
  1827 NE Forty-Fourth Ave.
  Portland, OR 97213
  Tel: 503-281-4181 *Fax:* 503-281-6739

Portland Community College
  Medical Assistant Prgm.
  12000 SW Forty-Ninth Ave.
  Portland, OR 97219
  Tel: 503-978-5665 *Fax:* 503-978-5257
  E-mail: drigsbee@pcc.edu

Chemeketa Community College
  Medical Assistant Prgm.
  P.O. Box 14007
  Salem, OR 97309
  Tel: 503-399-3994
  E-mail: bettyb@chemk.cc.or.us

Pennsylvania

Butler County Commmunity College
  Medical Assistant Prgm.
  P.O. Box 1203
  Butler, PA 16003-1203
  Tel: 412-287-8711, ext. 373
  Fax: 412-285-6047

Mt. Aloysius College
  Medical Assistant Prgm.
  7373 Admiral Peary Hwy.
  Cresson, PA 16630-1999
  Tel: 814-886-4131 *Fax:* 814-886-2978

Keystone Job Corps. Center
  Medical Assistant Prgm.
  P.O. Box 37
  Foothills Dr.
  Drums, PA 18222-0037
  Tel: 717-788-0216 *Fax:* 717-788-1119

Delaware County Community College
  Medical Assistant Prgm.
  Rte. 252 and Media Line Rd.
  Media, PA 19063
  Tel: 610-359-5274 *Fax:* 610-359-7350

Career Training Academy, Inc.
  Medical Assistant Prgm.
  ExpoMart
  105 Mall Blvd./Ste. 301-W
  Monroeville, PA 15146
  Tel: 412-372-3900 *Fax:* 412-373-4262

Career Training Academy, Inc.
  Medical Assistant Prgm.
  703 Fifth Ave.
  New Kensington, PA 15068
  Tel: 412-337-1000 *Fax:* 412-335-7140

Bucks County Community College
  Medical Assistant Prgm.
  Newton, PA 18940
  Tel: 215-968-8346

Community College of Philadelphia
  Medical Assistant Prgm.
  1700 Spring Garden St.
  Philadelphia, PA 19130
  Tel: 215-751-8947 *Fax:* 215-751-8937

Thompson Learning Corporation
  Medical Assistant Prgm.
  3440 Market St./2nd Fl.
  Philadelphia, PA 19104
  Tel: 215-387-1530 *Fax:* 215-387-0106

Bradford School–Pittsburgh
  Medical Assistant Prgm.
  Gulf Tower/707 Grand St.
  Pittsburgh, PA 15219
  Tel: 412-391-6366

Community College of Allegheny
    County
  Medical Assistant Prgm.
  808 Ridge Ave.
  Pittsburgh, PA 15212
  Tel: 412-237-2614 *Fax:* 412-237-4521
  E-mail: gcammara@ccac.edu

Duffs Business Institute
  Medical Assistant Prgm.
  110 Ninth St.
  Pittsburgh, PA 15222
  Tel: 412-261-4530 *Fax:* 412-261-4546

ICM School of Business and Medical
    Careers
  Medical Assistant Prgm.
  10 Wood St.
  Pittsburgh, PA 15222
  Tel: 412-261-2647 *Fax:* 412-261-6491

Median School of Allied Health
    Careers
  Medical Assistant Prgm.
  125 Seventh St.
  Pittsburgh, PA 15222
  Tel: 412-391-0422 *Fax:* 412-232-4348

Sawyer School
Medical Assistant Prgm.
717 Liberty Ave.
Pittsburgh, PA 15222
Tel: 412-261-5700 *Fax:* 412-281-7269

Lehigh Carbon Community College
Medical Assistant Prgm.
4525 Education Park Dr.
Schnecksville, PA 18078-2598
Tel: 610-079-1516 *Fax:* 610-799-1527

Central Pennsylvania Business School
Medical Assistant Prgm.
Campus on College Hill
Summerdale, PA 17093
Tel: 717-728-2216 *Fax:* 717-732-5254

Laurel Business Institute
Medical Assistant Prgm.
11-15 Penn St.
Uniontown, PA 15401
Tel: 412-439-4900 *Fax:* 412-439-3607

Berks Technical Institute
Medical Assistant Prgm.
2205 Ridgewood Rd.
Wyomissing, PA 19610
Tel: 610-372-1722 *Fax:* 610-376-4684

South Carolina

Forrest Junior College
Medical Assistant Prgm.
601 E. River St.
Anderson, SC 29624
Tel: 864-225-7653 *Fax:* 864-261-7471
E-mail: forrestjc@clemson.
campus.mci.net

Trident Technical College
Medical Assistant Prgm.
P.O. Box 118067
Charleston, SC 29423-8067
Tel: 803-572-6103

Midlands Technical College
Medical Assistant Prgm.
P.O. Box 2408
Columbia, SC 29202
Tel: 803-822-3398 *Fax:* 803-822-3619
E-mail: robertsonmd@mtc.
mid.tec.sc.us

Orangeburg Calhoun Technical
College
Medical Assistant Prgm.
3250 St. Matthews Rd.
Orangeburg, SC 29118
Tel: 803-535-1346 *Fax:* 803-535-1388

South Dakota

National American University
Medical Assistant Prgm.
321 Kansas City St.
Rapid City, SD 57709
Tel: 605-394-4839 *Fax:* 605-394-4871

Lake Area Technical Institute
Medical Assistant Prgm.
230 Eleventh St. NE
Watertown, SD 57201
Tel: 605-882-5284 *Fax:* 605-882-6299
E-mail: latiinfo@lati.tec.sd.us

Tennessee

Miller–Motte Business College
Medical Assistant Prgm.
1820 Business Park Dr.
Clarksville, TN 37040
Tel: 615-553-0071 *Fax:* 615-552-2916

East Tennessee State University
Medical Assistant Prgm.
ETSU Nave Center/ 1000 West E St.
Elizabethton, TN 37643
Tel: 423-547-4905
Fax: 423-547-4921
E-mail: fosterb@etsuvax.etsu.tn.edu

Tennessee Technology
Center–Livingston
Medical Assistant Prgm.
740 High Tech. Dr./ P.O. Box 219
Livingston, TN 38570
Tel: 615-823-5525 *Fax:* 615-823-7484

Shelby State Community College
Medical Assistant Prgm.
P.O. Box 40568
Memphis, TN 38174-0568
Tel: 901-544-5407 *Fax:* 901-544-5391

Fugazzi College
Medical Assistant Prgm.
5042 Linbar Dr./Ste. 200
Nashville, TN 37211
Tel: 615-333-3344 *Fax:* 615-333-3429

Texas

Cisco Junior College
Medical Assistant Prgm.
Box 3 Rte. 3
Cisco, TX 76437
Tel: 254-442-2567 *Fax:* 254-442-2546

Richland College
Medical Assistant Prgm.
12800 Abrams Rd.
Dallas, TX 75243

El Paso Community College
Medical Assistant Prgm.
P.O. Box 20500
El Paso, TX 79998
Tel: 915-534-4139

Western Technical Institute
Medical Assistant Prgm.
4710 Alabama St.
El Paso, TX 79930
Tel: 915-566-9621

Bradford School
Medical Assistant Prgm.
4669 SW Frwy. #300
Houston, TX 77027
Tel: 713-629-1500 *Fax:* 713-629-0059

San Antonio College
Medical Assistant Prgm.
1300 San Pedro Ave.
San Antonio, TX 78284
Tel: 210-733-2437 *Fax:* 210-733-2907

Utah

Davis Applied Technology Center
Medical Assistant Prgm.
550 E. 300 S
Kaysville, UT 84037
Tel: 801-546-2441 *Fax:* 801-544-9098

American Institute of Medical/Dental
  Technology
Medical Assistant Prgm.
1675 N. Freedom Blvd./ Bldg. 9A
Provo, UT 84604
Tel: 801-377-2900 *Fax:* 801-375-3077

Latter Day Saints Business College
Medical Assistant Prgm.
411 E. South Temple
Salt Lake City, UT 84111
Tel: 801-524-8131 *Fax:* 801-524-1900
E-mail: edith@email.ldsbc.edu

Salt Lake Community College
Medical Assistant Prgm.
4600 S. Redwood Rd./ P.O. Box 30808
Salt Lake City, UT 84130
Tel: 801-957-4090 *Fax:* 801-957-4612

Utah Career College
Medical Assistant Prgm.
1144 W. 3300 S
Salt Lake City, UT 84119
Tel: 801-975-7000 *Fax:* 801-975-7872

Virginia

National Business College of
  Charlottesville
Medical Assistant Prgm.
1819 Emmet St.
Charlottesville, VA 22903
Tel: 804-295-0136 *Fax:* 804-979-8061

National Business College of Danville
Medical Assistant Prgm.
734 Main St.
Danville, VA 24541
Tel: 804-793-6822 *Fax:* 804-793-3634

Commonwealth College–Hampton
  College
Medical Assistant Prgm.
1120 W. Mercury Blvd.
Hampton, VA 23666-3309
Tel: 804-838-2122 *Fax:* 804-745-6884

Dominion Business School of
  Harrisonburg
Medical Assistant Prgm.
933 Reservoir St.
Harrisonburg, VA 22801
Tel: 540-433-6977 *Fax:* 540-433-3726

National Business College of
  Harrisonburg
Medical Assistant Prgm.
51-B Burgess Rd.
Harrisonburg, VA 22801
Tel: 540-432-0943 *Fax:* 540-432-1133

National Business College of
  Lynchburg
Medical Assistant Prgm.
104 Candlewood Ct.
Lynchburg, VA 24502
Tel: 804-239-3500 *Fax:* 804-239-3948

Commonwealth College– Richmond
  Campus
  Medical Assistant Prgm.
  8141 Hull Street Rd.
  Richmond, VA 23235-6411
  Tel: 804-745-2444 *Fax:* 804-745-6884

Dominion Business School of Roanoke
  Medical Assistant Prgm.
  5372 Fallowater Ln./Ste. B
  Roanoke, VA 24015
  Tel: 540-776-8321 *Fax:* 540-776-9420

National Business College
  Medical Assistant Prgm.
  P.O. Box 6400
  Roanoke, VA 24017-0400
  Tel: 540-986-1800 *Fax:* 540-986-1344

National Business College of Bluefield
  Medical Assistant Prgm.
  1813 E. Main St.
  Salem, VA 24153
  Tel: 540-326-3621 *Fax:* 540-322-5731

Commonwealth College–Virgina
  Beach Campus
  Medical Assistant Prgm.
  301 Centre Pointe Dr.
  Virginia Beach, VA 23462
  Tel: 757-499-7900 *Fax:* 757-499-9977

Tidewater Community College
  Medical Assistant Prgm.
  1700 College Crescent
  Virginia Beach, VA 23456
  Tel: 757-427-7252 *Fax:* 757-427-1338

Washington

Highline Community College
  Medical Assistant Prgm.
  P.O. Box 98000
  Des Moines, WA 98198-9800
  Tel: 206-878-3710, ext. 3493
  Fax: 206-870-3780
  E-mail: ctamparo@hcc.etc.c

Everett Community College
  Medical Assistant Prgm.
  801 Wetmore
  Everett, WA 98201
  Tel: 206-388-9362 *Fax:* 206-388-9129

Lake Washington Technical College
  Medical Assistant Prgm.
  11605 132nd Ave. NE
  Kirkland, WA 98034-8506
  Tel: 425-739-8361 *Fax:* 425-739-8293
  E-mail: vnye@ctc.edu

Lower Columbia College
  Medical Assistant Prgm.
  1600 Maple St.
  Longview, WA 98622
  Tel: 360-578-1485 *Fax:* 360-577-3400

South Puget Sound Community
  College
  Medical Assistant Prgm.
  2011 Mottman Rd. SW
  Olympia, WA 98502-6218
  Tel: 360-754-7711, ext. 256
  Fax: 360-664-0780

North Seattle Community College
  Medical Assistant Prgm.
  9600 College Way N
  Seattle, WA 98103
  Tel: 206-525-4561 *Fax:* 206-527-3784
  E-mail: dbedford@nsccgate.
  sccd.ctc.edu

Wisconsin

Lakeshore Technical College
  Medical Assistant Prgm.
  1290 North Ave.
  Cleveland, WI 53015
  Tel: 414-458-4183

Gateway Technical College
  Medical Assistant Prgm.
  400 County Rd. H
  Elkhorn, WI 53121
  Tel: 414-741-6802 *Fax:* 414-741-6148

Northeast Wisconsin Technical College
  Medical Assistant Prgm.
  2740 W. Mason St./ P.O. Box 19042
  Green Bay, WI 54307-9042
  Tel: 920-498-5523 *Fax:* 920-498-5673

Blackhawk Technical College
  Medical Assistant Prgm.
  6004 Prairie Rd./ P.O. Box 53547
  Janesville, WI 53547
  Tel: 608-757-7608

Western Wisconsin Technical College
Medical Assistant Prgm.
304 N. Sixth St./P.O. Box 908
La Crosse, WI 54602-0908
Tel: 608-785-9922 *Fax:* 608-785-9407
E-mail: napoli@al.western.tec.wi.us

Madison Area Technical College
Medical Assistant Prgm.
3550 Anderson St.
Madison, WI 53791-9674
Tel: 608-246-6110 *Fax:* 608-246-6013
E-mail: sbuboltz@madison.tec.wi.us

Mid–State Technical College
Medical Assistant Prgm.
2600 W. Fifth St.
Marshfield, WI 54449
Tel: 715-387-2538 *Fax:* 715-389-2864

Concordia University Wisconsin
Medical Assistant Prgm.
12800 N. Lake Shore Dr.
Mequon, WI 53097
Tel: 414-243-4362 *Fax:* 414-243-4438
E-mail: rslota@bach.cuw.edu

Milwaukee Area Technical College
Medical Assistant Prgm.
700 W. State St.
Milwaukee, WI 53233
Tel: 414-297-6934 *Fax:* 414-297-6851

Stratton College
Medical Assistant Prgm.
1300 N. Jackson St.
Milwaukee, WI 53202
Tel: 414-276-5200 *Fax:* 414-276-3930

Wisconsin Indianhead Technical
College
Medical Assistant Prgm.
1019 S. Knowles Ave.
New Richmond, WI 54017
Tel: 715-246-6561 *Fax:* 715-246-2777

Waukesha County Technical College
Medical Assistant Prgm.
800 Main St.
Pewaukee, WI 53072
Tel: 414-691-5563 *Fax:* 414-691-5451
E-mail: kbraaten@waukesha. tec.wi.us

Gateway Technical College
Medical Assistant Prgm.
1001 S. Main St.
Racine, WI 53403
Tel: 414-631-7353 *Fax:* 414-631-1044

Nicolet Area Technical College
Medical Assistant Prgm.
P.O. Box 518
Rhinelander, WI 54501
Tel: 715-365-4539 *Fax:* 715-365-4542

EMERGENCY MEDICAL TECHNICIAN–PARAMEDIC TRAINING PROGRAMS

Alabama

Gadsden State Community College
Emergency Med. Tech–Paramedic
Prgm.
P.O. Box 263
Anniston, AL 36202-0263
Tel: 205-235-5674 *Fax:* 205-235-5600

University of Alabama at Birmingham
Emergency Med. Tech–Paramedic
Prgm.
Dept. of Emergency Medicine
912 Eighteenth St. So
Birmingham, AL 35205
Tel: 205-934-3611 *Fax:* 205-934-5980

George C. Wallace State Community
College
Emergency Med. Tech–Paramedic
Prgm.
Dept. of Emergency Medicine
Dothan, AL 36303
Tel: 334-983-3521 *Fax:* 334-983-4255

Wallace State College
Emergency Med. Tech–Paramedic
Prgm.
301 Main St. NW/P.O. Box 2000
Hanceville, AL 35077
Tel: 205-352-8000 *Fax:* 205-352-8228

University of Alabama at
Birmingham–Huntsville
Emergency Med. Tech–Paramedic
Prgm.
109 Governors Dr. SW
Huntsville, AL 35801
Tel: 205-551-4416 *Fax:* 205-551-4451
E-mail: beckr@email.uah.edu

University of South Alabama
Emergency Med. Tech–Paramedic
Prgm.
2002 Old Bay Front Dr.
Mobile, AL 36615
Tel: 334-431-6418 *Fax:* 334-431-6525
E-mail: ecarlson@usouthal.campus.
mci.net

H. Councill Trenholm State Technical
College
Emergency Med. Tech–Paramedic
Prgm.
1225 Air Base Blvd.
Montgomery, AL 36108
Tel: 334-240-9674 *Fax:* 334-832-9777

Southern Union State Community
College
Emergency Med. Tech–Paramedic
Prgm.
1701 LaFayette Pkwy.
Opelika, AL 36801
Tel: 334-745-6437

Shelton State Community College/
Alabama Fire College
Emergency Med. Tech–Paramedic
Prgm.
2015 McFarland Blvd. E.
Tuscaloosa, AL 35405
Tel: 205-391-3754 *Fax:* 205-391-3747

California

Daniel Freeman Memorial Hospital
Emergency Med. Tech–Paramedic
Prgm.
333 N. Prairie Ave.
Inglewood, CA 90301
Tel: 310-674-7050 *Fax:* 310-419-8256
E-mail: cigallagher@compuserve.com

Crafton Hills College
Emergency Med. Tech–Paramedic
Prgm.
11711 Sand Canyon Rd.
Yucaipa, CA 92399
Tel: 909-389-3251 *Fax:* 909-389-3256

Colorado

Provenant–St. Anthony Hospitals
Emergency Med. Tech–Paramedic
Prgm.
Sixteenth and Raleigh Sts.
Denver, CO 80204
Tel: 303-629-3975

Swedish Medical Center
Emergency Med. Tech–Paramedic
Prgm.
Columbia Colorado Division
300 E. Hampden Ave., #100m
Englewood, CO 80110
Tel: 303-788-6302 *Fax:* 303-788-7656

Colorado Association of Paramedical
Education, Inc.
Emergency Med. Tech–Paramedic
Prgm.
9191 Grant St.
Thornton, CO 80229
Tel: 303-450-4436 *Fax:* 303-450-4458

Connecticut

CCTC/St. Francis Hospital & Medical
Center
Emergency Med. Tech–Paramedic
Prgm.
61 Woodland St.
Hartford, CT 06105-2354
Tel: 860-520-7872 *Fax:* 860-520-7906
E-mail: devito@commnet.eudu

Delaware

Kent General Central Delaware's
Hospital
Emergency Med. Tech–Paramedic
Prgm.
640 S. State Street
Dover, DE 19901
Tel: 302-674-7200 *Fax:* 302-674-7984
E-mail: banepon@aol.com

Medical Center of Delaware
Emergency Med. Tech–Paramedic
Prgm.
501 W. Fourteenth St.
P.O. Box 1668
Wilmington, DE 19899
Tel: 302-428-2913 *Fax:* 302-428-2797

Florida

Manatee Technical Institute
Emergency Med. Tech–Paramedic
Prgm.
5603 Thirty-Fourth St. W.
Bradenton, FL 34210
Tel: 941-751-7977 *Fax:* 941-751-7927

Brevard Community College
Emergency Med. Tech–Paramedic
Prgm.
1519 Clearlake Rd.
Cocoa, FL 32922
Tel: 407-632-1111, ext. 64175
Fax: 407-634-3731
E-mail:
robinson.meli@brevard.cc.fl.us

Daytona Beach Community College
Emergency Med. Tech–Paramedic
Prgm.
P.O. Box 2811
Daytona Beach, FL 32120-2811
Tel: 904-255-8131 *Fax:* 904-254-4491
E-mail: scalesd@dbcc.cc.fl.us

Lake County Vocational Technical
College
Emergency Med. Tech–Paramedic
Prgm.
2001 Kurt St.
Eustis, FL 32726
Tel: 352-383-2555 *Fax:* 352-735-3013

Broward Community College
Emergency Med. Tech–Paramedic
Prgm.
3501 SW Davis Rd./Bldg. 8
Ft. Lauderdale, FL 33314
Tel: 954-475-6776 *Fax:* 954-473-9037

Edison Community College
Emergency Med. Tech–Paramedic
Prgm.
8099 College Pkwy. SW/P.O. Box
06210
Ft. Myers, FL 33906-6210
Tel: 941-489-9108 *Fax:* 941-489-9331

Indian River Community College
Emergency Med. Tech–Paramedic
Prgm.
3209 Virginia Ave.
Ft. Pierce, FL 34981-5599
Tel: 561-462-4471

Santa Fe Community College
Emergency Med. Tech–Paramedic
Prgm.
3000 NW Eighty-third St./Bldg.
W201-I
Gainesville, FL 32606-6200
Tel: 352-395-5755 *Fax:* 352-395-5711
E-mail: gail.stewart@santafe.cc.fl.us

Florida Community
    College–Jacksonville
Emergency Med. Tech–Paramedic
    Prgm.
North Campus/4501 Capper Rd.
Jacksonville, FL 32218
Tel: 904-766-6513 *Fax:* 904-766-6654

Lake City Community College
Emergency Med. Tech–Paramedic
    Prgm.
Rte. 19 Box 1030
Lake City, FL 32025
Tel: 904-752-1822, ext. 1149
Fax: 904-758-9959

Palm Beach Community College
Emergency Med. Tech–Paramedic
    Prgm.
4200 S. Congress Ave.
Lake Worth, FL 33461
Tel: 561-439-8260 *Fax:* 561-439-8202
E-mail: alshusband@msn.com

Miami–Dade Community College
Emergency Med. Tech–Paramedic
    Prgm.
Medical Center Campus
950 NW Twentieth St.
Miami, FL 33127
Tel: 305-237-4038 *Fax:* 305-237-4278
E-mail: dbaralo@mdcc.edu

Pasco–Hernando Community College
Emergency Med. Tech–Paramedic
    Prgm.
10230 Ridge Rd.
New Port Richey, FL 34654-5199
Tel: 813-847-2727 *Fax:* 813-816-3300

Central Florida Community College
Emergency Med. Tech–Paramedic
    Prgm.
P.O. Box 1388
Ocala, FL 34478
Tel: 352-237-2111

Valencia Community College
Emergency Med. Tech–Paramedic
    Prgm.
P.O. Box 3028
Orlando, FL 32802-9961
Tel: 407-299-5000 *Fax:* 407-293-8839

Gulf Coast Community College
Emergency Med. Tech–Paramedic
    Prgm.
5230 W. U.S. Hwy. 98
Panama City, FL 32401
Tel: 850-913-3315 *Fax:* 850-747-3246
E-mail: dfinley@ccmail.gc.cc.fl.us

Pensacola Junior College
Emergency Med. Tech–Paramedic
    Prgm.
Warrington Campus
5555 W. Hwy. 98
Pensacola, FL 32507-1097
Tel: 904-484-2215 *Fax:* 904-484-2365

St. Petersburg Junior College
Emergency Med. Tech–Paramedic
    Prgm.
Health Education Center
7200 Sixty-sixth St. N.
Pinellas Park, FL 33565
Tel: 813-341-3656 *Fax:* 813-341-3655
E-mail:
    stepanovskyn@email.spjc.cc.fl.us

Seminole Community College
Emergency Med. Tech–Paramedic
    Prgm.
100 Weldon Blvd.
Sanford, FL 32773
Tel: 407-328-2198
Fax: 407-328-2139

Sarasota County Institute Center
Emergency Med. Tech–Paramedic
    Prgm.
4748 Beneva Rd.
Sarasota, FL 34233
Tel: 941-924-1365 *Fax:* 941-361-6886

St. Augustine Technical Center
Emergency Med. Tech–Paramedic
    Prgm.
2980 Collins Ave.
St. Augustine, FL 32095-9970
Tel: 904-829-1080 *Fax:* 904-824-6750

Tallahassee Community College
Emergency Med. Tech–Paramedic
    Prgm.
444 Appleyard Dr.
Tallahassee, FL 32304
Tel: 904-922-8156 *Fax:* 904-921-5722
E-mail:
    dunmyerb@mail.tallahassee.cc.fl.us

Hillsborough Community College
Emergency Med. Tech–Paramedic
Prgm.
P.O. Box 30030
Tampa, FL 33630
Tel: 813-253-7454   *Fax:* 813-253-7464

Polk Community College
Emergency Med. Tech–Paramedic
Prgm.
999 Ave. H NE
Winter Haven, FL 33881-4299
Tel: 941-297-1000   *Fax:* 941-297-1010
E-mail: cstory@mail.polk.cc.fl.us

Illinois

Foster G. McGaw Hospital of Loyola
University
Emergency Med. Tech–Paramedic
Prgm.
2160 S. First Ave.
Maywood, IL 60153
Tel: 708-327-2544   *Fax:* 708-327-2548

Trinity Medical Center
Emergency Med. Tech–Paramedic
Prgm.
501 Tenth Ave.
Moline, IL 61265
Tel: 309-757-3168   *Fax:* 309-757-3138

Indiana

Ivy Tech State College SW–Evansville
Emergency Med. Tech–Paramedic
Prgm.
3501 First Ave.
Evansville, IN 47710
Tel: 812-428-0850   *Fax:* 812-429-1383

Methodist Hospital of Indiana, Inc.
Emergency Med. Tech–Paramedic
Prgm.
1701 N. Senate Blvd.
Indianapolis, IN 46206
Tel: 317-929-3785

Iowa

Mercy College of Health Sciences
Emergency Med. Tech–Paramedic
Prgm.
School of EMS
Des Moines, IA 50309-1239
Tel: 515-247-4097   *Fax:* 515-362-6698
E-mail: mercy@mchs.edu

Kansas

Johnson County Community College
Emergency Med. Tech–Paramedic
Prgm.
12345 College Blvd.
Overland Park, KS 66210-1299
Tel: 913-469-8500   *Fax:* 913-469-2315
E-mail: dkurogi@johnco.cc.ks.us

Kentucky

Eastern Kentucky University
Emergency Med. Tech–Paramedic
Prgm.
Dizney 225
Richmond, KY 40475-3135
Tel: 606-622-1028   *Fax:* 606-622-1140
E-mail: mtscreme@acs.eku.edu

Louisiana

University of Southwestern Louisiana
Emergency Med. Tech–Paramedic
Prgm.
P.O. Drawer 41008
Lafayette, LA 70504
Tel: 318-482-5603   *Fax:* 318-482-5649
E-mail: smg3846@usl.edu

Maryland

University of Maryland Baltimore
County
Emergency Med. Tech–Paramedic
Prgm.
Emergency Health Services Dept.
1000 Hilltop Circle
Baltimore, MD 21250
Tel: 410-455-3223   *Fax:* 410-455-3045
E-mail: polk@umbc.edu

Michigan

Lansing Community College
Emergency Med. Tech–Paramedic
Prgm.
500 N. Washington/P.O. Box 40010
Lansing, MI 48901-7210
Tel: 517-483-1410

Minnesota

Northwest Technical College–East
   Grand Forks
   Emergency Med. Tech–Paramedic
      Prgm.
   P.O. Box 111 Hwy. 220 N.
   East Grand Forks, MN 56721
   Tel: 218-773-3411 *Fax:* 218-773-4502
   E-mail: sponsler@adm.egf.tec.mn.us

Century Community and Technical
   College
   Emergency Med. Tech–Paramedic
      Prgm.
   3300 Century Ave. N.
   White Bear Lake, MN 55110
   Tel: 612-779-5794 *Fax:* 612-779-5779

Mississippi

Jones County Junior College
   Emergency Med. Tech–Paramedic
      Prgm.
   900 S. Court St.
   Ellisville, MS 39437
   Tel: 601-477-4074 *Fax:* 601-477-4152

Itawamba Community College
   Emergency Med. Tech–Paramedic
      Prgm.
   602 W. Hill St.
   Fulton, MS 38843
   Tel: 601-862-3101 *Fax:* 601-862-4614

Forrest General Hospital
   Emergency Med. Tech–Paramedic
      Prgm.
   6051 U.S. Hwy. 49 S.
   Hattiesburg, MS 39401
   Tel: 601-288-2655 *Fax:* 601-288-2668

University of Mississippi Medical
   Center
   Emergency Med. Tech–Paramedic
      Prgm.
   2500 N. State St.
   Jackson, MS 39216
   Tel: 601-984-5585 *Fax:* 601-984-6768

Mississippi Gulf Coast Community
   College
   Emergency Med. Tech–Paramedic
      Prgm.
   2226 Switzer Rd.
   Long Beach, MS 39560
   Tel: 601-896-2554 *Fax:* 601-896-2520

Southwestern Mississippi Regional
   Medical Center
   Emergency Med. Tech–Paramedic
      Prgm.
   P.O. Box 1307
   McComb, MS 39648
   Tel: 601-684-5163

Missouri

St. Louis University Medical Center/
   Barnes Hospital
   Emergency Med. Tech–Paramedic
      Prgm.
   IHM Hlth. Studies Ctr./2500 Abbott Pl.
   St. Louis, MO 63143
   Tel: 314-768-1234 *Fax:* 314-768-1595

Nebraska

Creighton University
   Emergency Med. Tech–Paramedic
      Prgm.
   Pre-Hospital Educ./2514 Cuming St.
   Omaha, NE 68131
   Tel: 402-280-1280 *Fax:* 402-280-1288
   E-mail: dwackher@creighton.edu

New Hampshire

New Hampshire Technical Institute
   Emergency Med. Tech–Paramedic
      Prgm.
   11 Institute Dr.
   Concord, NH 03001-7412
   Tel: 603-225-1836 *Fax:* 603-225-1895

Elliot Hospital/Catholic Medical
   Center
   Emergency Med. Tech–Paramedic
      Prgm.
   Dept. of EMS/Trauma Svcs.
   One Elliot Way
   Manchester, NH 03103
   Tel: 603-628-2641 *Fax:* 603-628-2110
   E-mail: bglea12206@aol.com

New Mexico

University of New Mexico School of
   Medicine
   Emergency Med. Tech–Paramedic
      Prgm.
   School of Medicine/2700 Yale Blvd.
      SE
   Albuquerque, NM 87106
   Tel: 505-272-5757 *Fax:* 505-244-1505

Donas Ana Branch Community
    College
Emergency Med. Tech–Paramedic
    Prgm.
Box 30001/Dept. 3DA
Las Cruces, NM 88003
Tel: 505-527-7645 *Fax:* 505-527-7515
E-mail: Cosborn@nmsu.edu

Eastern New Mexico
    University–Roswell
Emergency Med. Tech–Paramedic
    Prgm.
P.O. Box 6000
Roswell, NM 88202
Tel: 505-624-7239 *Fax:* 505-624-7100
E-mail:
    buldran@hib.enmuros.cc.nm.us

New York

CUNY Borough of Manhattan
    Community College
Emergency Med. Tech–Paramedic
    Prgm.
199 Chambers St.
Dept. of Allied Hlth. Sciences
New York, NY 10007
Tel: 212-346-8734 *Fax:* 212-346-8730

North Carolina

Western Carolina University
Emergency Med. Tech–Paramedic
    Prgm.
Cullowhee, NC 28723
Tel: 704-227-7113 *Fax:* 704-227-7446
E-mail: mhubble@wcuvax.wcu.edu

Catawba Valley Community College
Emergency Med. Tech–Paramedic
    Prgm.
2550 Hwy. 70 SE
Hickory, NC 28602-9699
Tel: 704-327-7276 *Fax:* 704-327-7276
E-mail: mmccrea@cvcc.cc.nc.us

Ohio

Akron General Medical Center
Emergency Med. Tech–Paramedic
    Prgm.
400 Wabash Ave.
Akron, OH 44307
Tel: 330-384-6655 *Fax:* 330-996-2300

University of Cincinnati Hospital
Emergency Med. Tech–Paramedic
    Prgm.
231 Bethesda Ave.
Cincinnati, OH 45267-0769
Tel: 513-558-8093 *Fax:* 513-558-5719

Columbus State Community College
Emergency Med. Tech–Paramedic
    Prgm.
550 E. Spring St.
Columbus, OH 43215
Tel: 614-227-2510 *Fax:* 614-227-5744

Parma Community General Hospital
Emergency Med. Tech–Paramedic
    Prgm.
7300 State Rd.
Parma, OH 44134
Tel: 440-886-7323 *Fax:* 440-886-1295

Youngstown State University
Emergency Med. Tech–Paramedic
    Prgm.
1 University Plaza
Youngstown, OH 44555
Tel: 330-742-3327 *Fax:* 330-742-2921
E-mail: rwbenner@cc.ysu.edu

Oregon

College of Emergency Services
Emergency Med. Tech–Paramedic
    Prgm.
9735 SW Sunshine Ct., #700
Beaverton, OR 97005
Tel: 503-644-9999 *Fax:* 503-644-1672

Oregon Health Sciences University
Emergency Med. Tech–Paramedic
    Prgm.
Dept. of Emer. Med.–Gaines Hall–Rm.
    239
3181 SW Sam Jackson Pk. Rd.
Portland, OR 97201
Tel: 503-494-8586 *Fax:* 503-494-1470
E-mail: saitoj@ohsu.edu

Pennsylvania

Harrisburg Area Community College
Emergency Med. Tech–Paramedic
    Prgm.
One HACC Dr.
Harrisburg, PA 17110-2999
Tel: 717-780-2564 *Fax:* 717-780-2551
E-mail: cadavis@hacc01b.hacc.edu

Center for Emergency Medicine of
    Western Pennsylvania
    Emergency Med. Tech–Paramedic
      Prgm.
    230 McKee Pl./Ste. 500
    Pittsburgh, PA 15213
    Tel: 412-578-3200 *Fax:* 412-578-3241

Williamsport Hospital
    Emergency Med. Tech–Paramedic
      Prgm.
    777 Rural Ave.
    Williamsport, PA 17701
    Tel: 717-321-2387 *Fax:* 717-321-2263
    E-mail: twhmcpti@csrlink.net

South Carolina

Greenville Technical College
    Emergency Med. Tech–Paramedic
      Prgm.
    P.O. Box 5616 Station B
    Greenville, SC 29606
    Tel: 864-250-8218 *Fax:* 864-250-8462
    E-mail: cothrackc@gvltec.edu

Tennessee

Northeast State Technical Community
    College
    Emergency Med. Tech–Paramedic
      Prgm.
    P.O. Box 246
    Blountville, TN 37617-0246
    Tel: 423-323-0238 *Fax:* 423-323-3083
    E-mail: dscoleman@nstcc.cc.tn.us

Volunteer State Community College
    Emergency Med. Tech–Paramedic
      Prgm.
    1480 Nashville Pike
    Gallatin, TN 37066
    Tel: 615-230-3346 *Fax:* 615-230-3344
    E-mail: rcollier@vscc.cc.tn.us

Roane State Community College
    Emergency Med. Tech–Paramedic
      Prgm.
    Harriman, TN 37748
    Tel: 423-539-6905 *Fax:* 423-539-6907

Jackson State Community College
    Emergency Med. Tech–Paramedic
      Prgm.
    2046 N. Parkway St.
    Jackson, TN 38301-3797
    Tel: 901-424-3520 *Fax:* 901-425-2647
    E-mail: tcoley@jscc.cc.tn.us

Shelby State Community College
    Emergency Med. Tech–Paramedic
      Prgm.
    P.O. Box 40568
    Memphis, TN 38174-0568
    Tel: 901-544-5412 *Fax:* 901-544-5391
    E-mail: Foon@sscc.cc.Tn.us

Texas

Austin Community College
    Emergency Med. Tech–Paramedic
      Prgm.
    1020 Grove Blvd.
    Austin, TX 78741
    Tel: 512-223-6112 *Fax:* 512-369-6700
    E-mail: jhayes@flash.net

Lee College
    Emergency Med. Tech–Paramedic
      Prgm.
    P.O. Box 818
    Baytown, TX 77522-0818
    Tel: 281-425-6836
    E-mail: ewhitene@lee.edu

University of Texas Southwestern
    Medical Center–Dallas
    Emergency Med. Tech–Paramedic
      Prgm.
    5323 Harry Hines Blvd.
    Dallas, TX 75235-8890
    Tel: 214-648-3131 *Fax:* 214-648-7580
    E-mail: dcason@mednet.swmed.edu

Houston Community College Central
    Emergency Med. Tech–Paramedic
      Prgm.
    6815 Rustic
    Houston, TX 77087
    Tel: 713-718-7606 *Fax:* 713-718-7098

Texas Technical University Health
    Sciences Center
    Emergency Med. Tech–Paramedic
      Prgm.
    3601 Fourth St.
    Lubbock, TX 79430
    Tel: 806-743-3218 *Fax:* 806-743-1315
    E-mail: alhnbc@ttuhsc.edu

University of Texas Health Sciences
    Center at San Antonio
    Emergency Med. Tech–Paramedic
    Prgm.
    7703 Floyd Curl Dr.
    San Antonio, TX 78284
    Tel: 210-567-7860 *Fax:* 210-567-7887
    E-mail: garoni@uthscsa.edu

College of the Mainland
    Emergency Med. Tech–Paramedic
    Prgm.
    1200 Amburn Rd.
    Texas City, TX 77591
    Tel: 409-938-1211, Ext. 255
    Fax: 409-938-1211
    E-mail: neubanks@campus.mainland.
    cc.tx.us

Utah

Weber State University
    Emergency Med. Tech–Paramedic
    Prgm.
    Ogden, UT 84408-3902
    Tel: 801-626-6521 *Fax:* 801-626-6610
    E-mail: vquick\@weber.edu

Virginia

Northern Virginia Community College
    Emergency Med. Tech–Paramedic
    Prgm.
    8333 Little River Trnpk.
    Annandale, VA 22003
    Tel: 703-323-3037 *Fax:* 703-323-4576

College of Health Sciences
    Emergency Med. Tech–Paramedic
    Prgm.
    P.O. Box 13186
    Roanoke, VA 24031-3186
    Tel: 540-985-8398 *Fax:* 540-985-9773

Washington

Central Washington University
    Emergency Med. Tech–Paramedic
    Prgm.
    Dept. of Physical Educ.
    Hlth. Education & Leisure Services
    Ellensburg, WA 98926
    Tel: 509-963-1451 *Fax:* 509-963-1848

Harborview Medical
    Center–University of Washington
    Emergency Med. Tech–Paramedic
    Prgm.
    325 Ninth Avenue/Mailbox 359727
    Seattle, WA 98104
    Tel: 206-731-3489 *Fax:* 206-731-8554
    E-mail: rwaugh@u.washington.edu

Spokane Community College
    Emergency Med. Tech–Paramedic
    Prgm.
    N. 1810 Greene St.
    Spokane, WA 99217
    Tel: 509-533-7296 *Fax:* 509-533-8621
    E-mail: msesso@clc.ctc.edu

Tacoma Community College
    Emergency Med. Tech–Paramedic
    Prgm.
    6501 S. Nineteenth St.
    Tacoma, WA 98466
    Tel: 206-566-5220 *Fax:* 206-566-5273

PHYSICAL THERAPIST ASSISTANT TRAINING PROGRAMS

Alabama

Wallace State College
Physical Therapist Assistant Prgm.
P.O. Box 2000
Hanceville, AL 35077-2000
Tel: 205-352-8332 *Fax:* 205-352-8320

Bishop State Community College
Physical Therapist Assistant Prgm.
1365 Martin Luther King Ave.
Mobile, AL 36603-5362
Tel: 334-405-4441 *Fax:* 334-405-4427

Arizona

Gateway Community College
Physical Therapist Assistant Prgm.
108 N. Fortieth St.
Phoenix, AZ 85034
Tel: 602-392-5336 *Fax:* 602-392-5300

Arkansas

Northwest Arkansas Community
College
Physical Therapist Assistant Prgm.
One College Dr.
Bentonville, AR 72712-5091
Tel: 501-619-4153 *Fax:* 501-939-5117

University of Central Arkansas
Physical Therapist Assistant Prgm.
Dept. of Physical Therapy
Conway, AR 72035-0001
Tel: 501-450-5548

California

De Anza College
Physical Therapist Assistant Prgm.
21250 Stevens Creek Blvd.
Cupertino, CA 95014
Tel: 408-864-8687 *Fax:* 408-864-5630

Loma Linda University
Physical Therapist Assistant Prgm.
School of Allied Health Professions
Nichol Hall Rm. 1911
Loma Linda, CA 92350
Tel: 909-824-4634 *Fax:* 909-824-4291
E-mail: dtaylor@sahp.llu.edu

Mt. St. Mary's College
Physical Therapist Assistant Prgm.
10 Chester Pl.
Los Angeles, CA 90007
Tel: 213-477-2600 *Fax:* 213-477-2609

Cerritos College
Physical Therapist Assistant Prgm.
Health Occupations Div.
11110 Alondra Blvd.
Norwalk, CA 90650
Tel: 562-860-2451, ext. 2550
Fax: 562-467-5077

Sacramento City College
Physical Therapist Assistant Prgm.
Allied Health
3835 Freeport Blvd.
Sacramento, CA 95822
Tel: 916-558-2240 *Fax:* 916-558-2392
E-mail:
chapeb@mail.scc.losrios.cc.ca.us

San Diego Mesa College
Physical Therapist Assistant Prgm.
7250 Mesa College Dr.
San Diego, CA 92111-4998
Tel: 619-627-2839 *Fax:* 619-279-5668

Professional Skills Institute/Santa
Barbara Campus
Physical Therapist Assistant Prgm.
4213 State St./Ste. 302
Santa Barbara, CA 93110
Tel: 805-683-1902 *Fax:* 805-683-6372

Colorado

Denver Technical College
Physical Therapist Assistant Prgm.
925 S. Niagara St.
Denver, CO 80224
Tel: 303-329-3340, ext. 259
Fax: 303-322-0386

Morgan Community College
Physical Therapist Assistant Prgm.
17800 Rd. 20
Ft. Morgan, CO 80701
Tel: 800-622-0216 *Fax:* 970-867-9121

Arapahoe Community College
Physical Therapist Assistant Prgm.
2500 W. College Dr./P.O. Box 9002
Littleton, CO 80160-9002
Tel: 303-797-5897 *Fax:* 303-797-5935

Pueblo Community College
Physical Therapist Assistant Prgm.
900 W. Orman Ave.
Pueblo, CO 81004
Tel: 719-549-3280 *Fax:* 719-549-3136

Connecticut

Housatonic Community Technical
College
Physical Therapist Assistant Prgm.
900 Lafayette Blvd.
Bridgeport, CT 06604-4704
Tel: 203-332-5000 *Fax:* 203-332-5123

Delaware

Delaware Technical & Community
College–Owens Campus
Physical Therapist Assistant Prgm.
P.O. Box 610
Georgetown, DE 19947
Tel: 302-856-5400 *Fax:* 302-856-5773

Delaware Technical & Community
College–Wilmington
Physical Therapist Assistant Prgm.
333 Shipley St.
Wilmington, DE 19801
Tel: 302-571-5355 *Fax:* 302-577-2548

Florida

Lynn University
Physical Therapist Assistant Prgm.
3601 N. Military Trail
Boca Raton, FL 33431-5598
Tel: 561-994-0770, ext. 310
Fax: 561-989-4981

Broward Community College
Physical Therapist Assistant Prgm.
Ctr. for Health Science Education
3501 SW Davie Rd./Bldg. 8
Fort Lauderdale, FL 33314
Tel: 954-969-2086 *Fax:* 954-973-2348

Lake City Community College
Physical Therapist Assistant Prgm.
Rte. 19 Box 1030
Lake City, FL 32025
Tel: 904-752-1822, ext. 1143
Fax: 904-758-9959

Miami–Dade Community College
Physical Therapist Assistant Prgm.
MDCC Medical Campus
950 NW Twentieth St.
Miami, FL 33127
Tel: 305-237-4141 *Fax:* 305-237-4116

Central Florida Community College
Physical Therapist Assistant Prgm.
P.O. Box 1388
Ocala, FL 34478-1388
Tel: 352-854-2322, ext. 255
Fax: 352-237-0510

Seminole Community College
Physical Therapist Assistant Prgm.
100 Weldon Blvd.
Sanford, FL 32773-6199
Tel: 407-328-2235 *Fax:* 407-328-2139

St. Petersburg Junior College
Physical Therapist Assistant Prgm.
P.O. Box 13489
St. Petersburg, FL 33733
Tel: 813-341-3611 *Fax:* 813-341-3744
E-mail: ericksond@email.spjc.cc.fl.us

Pensacola Junior College
Physical Therapist Assistant Prgm.
Warrington Campus
5555 W. Hwy. 98
Warrington, FL 32507
Tel: 904-484-2301 *Fax:* 904-484-2365

Polk Community College
Physical Therapist Assistant Prgm.
999 Avenue H NE
Winter Haven, FL 33881
Tel: 941-297-1020, ext. 5641

Georgia

Darton College
Physical Therapist Assistant Prgm.
2400 Gillionville Rd.
Albany, GA 31707
Tel: 912-430-6000 *Fax:* 912-430-6095

Gwinnett Technical Institute
Physical Therapist Assistant Prgm.
5150 Sugarloaf Pkwy.
Lawrenceville, GA 30245
Tel: 770-962-7580 *Fax:* 770-962-7985
E-mail: spalma@gwinnett.tec.ga.us

Thomas Technical Institute
Physical Therapist Assistant Prgm.
15689 U.S. Hwy. 19N
Thomasville, GA 31792
Tel: 912-225-4098 *Fax:* 912-225-5289

Hawaii

Kapiolani Community College
  Physical Therapist Assistant Prgm.
  4303 Diamond Head Rd.
  Honolulu, HI 96816
  Tel: 808-734-9350 *Fax:* 808-734-9126
  E-mail: marilynm@hawaii.edu

Illinois

Belleville Area College
  Physical Therapist Assistant Prgm.
  2500 Carlyle Rd.
  Belleville, IL 62221
  Tel: 618-235-2700, ext. 362
  Fax: 618-235-1578

Southern Illinois University
  Physical Therapist Assistant Prgm.
  SIU Clinical Ctr.
  Clinical Center-4602
  Carbondale, IL 62901-4602
  Tel: 618-453-6143 *Fax:* 618-453-6126

Kaskaskia College
  Physical Therapist Assistant Prgm.
  27210 College Rd.
  Centralia, IL 62801
  Tel: 618-532-1981, ext. 205
  Fax: 618-532-9792
  E-mail: srdewhirst@kccn.kc.cc.il.us

Morton College
  Physical Therapist Assistant Prgm.
  3801 S. Central Ave.
  Cicero, IL 60650
  Tel: 708-656-8000, ext. 380

Oakton Community College
  Physical Therapist Assistant Prgm.
  1600 E. Golf Rd.
  Des Plaines, IL 60016
  Tel: 847-635-1857 *Fax:* 847-635-1764
  E-mail: maryd@oakton.edu

Lake Land College
  Physical Therapist Assistant Prgm.
  LLC Kluthe Center
  1204 Network Center Dr.
  Effingham, IL 62401
  Tel: 217-342-0951 *Fax:* 217-342-0999

Black Hawk College
  Physical Therapist Assistant Prgm.
  6600 Thirty-Fourth Ave.
  Moline, IL 61265-5899
  Tel: 309-796-1311, ext. 3315
  Fax: 309-792-3418

Illinois Central College
  Physical Therapist Assistant Prgm.
  201 SW Adams St.
  Peoria, IL 61635-0001
  Tel: 309-999-4600 *Fax:* 309-673-9531

Lincoln Land Community College
  Physical Therapist Assistant Prgm.
  Lincoln Land Community College
  Shepherd Rd.
  Springfield, IL 62794-9256
  Tel: 217-786-2498 *Fax:* 217-786-2776

Indiana

University of Evansville
  Physical Therapist Assistant Prgm.
  1800 Lincoln Ave.
  Evansville, IN 47722
  Tel: 812-479-2341 *Fax:* 812-479-2717

University of Indianapolis
  Physical Therapist Assistant Prgm.
  Krannert School of Physical Therapy
  1400 E. Hanna Ave.
  Indianapolis, IN 46227-3697
  Tel: 317-788-3459 *Fax:* 317-788-3569
  E-mail: pritzline@gandlf.unidy.edu

Michiana College
  Physical Therapist Assistant Prgm.
  1030 E. Jefferson Blvd.
  South Bend, IN 46617
  Tel: 219-237-0774 *Fax:* 219-237-3585

Vincennes University
  Physical Therapist Assistant Prgm.
  Health Occupations Dept.
  Vincennes, IN 47591
  Tel: 812-888-4416 *Fax:* 812-888-5868

Iowa

Kirkwood Community College
  Physical Therapist Assistant Prgm.
  6301 Kirkwood Blvd.
  Cedar Rapids, IA 52406
  Tel: 319-398-5566 *Fax:* 319-398-1293
  E-mail: mthomas@kirkwood.cc.ia.us

Indian Hills Community College
  Physical Therapist Assistant Prgm.
  Health Occupations Dept.
  Ottumwa Campus/525 Grandview
  Ottumwa, IA 52501
  Tel: 515-683-5164 *Fax:* 515-683-5184

Western Iowa Tech Community
  College
  Physical Therapist Assistant Prgm.
  4647 Stone Ave./P.O. Box 265
  Sioux City, IA 51102-5199
  Tel: 712-274-6400 *Fax:* 712-274-6412

Kansas

Colby Community College
  Physical Therapist Assistant Prgm.
  1255 South Range
  Colby, KS 67701
  Tel: 913-462-4797 *Fax:* 913-462-4699
  E-mail: wanda@katie.colby.cc.ks.us

Washburn University of Topeka
  Physical Therapist Assistant Prgm.
  School of Applied Studies
  1700 College Ave.
  Topeka, KS 66621
  Tel: 785-231-1010, ext. 1406
  Fax: 785-231-1027
  E-mail: zzbahn@pro.wuacc.edu

Wichita State University
  Physical Therapist Assistant Prgm.
  Dept. of Physical Therapy
  1845 N. Fairmount
  Wichita, KS 67260-0043
  Tel: 316-689-3604

Kentucky

Jefferson Community College
  Physical Therapist Assistant Prgm.
  109 E. Broadway St.
  Louisville, KY 40202-2005
  Tel: 502-584-0181, ext. 2201
  Fax: 502-585-4425

Madisonville Community College
  Physical Therapist Assistant Prgm.
  2000 College Dr.
  Madisonville, KY 42431-9185
  Tel: 502-821-2250, ext. 2175
  Fax: 502-821-1555

Paducah Community College
  Physical Therapist Assistant Prgm.
  P.O. Box 7380
  Paducah, KY 42002-7380
  Tel: 502-554-6274 *Fax:* 502-554-6227

Louisiana

Delgado Community College
  Physical Therapist Assistant Prgm.
  615 City Park Ave.
  New Orleans, LA 70119-4399
  Tel: 504-483-4035 *Fax:* 504-483-4609

Maine

Kennebec Valley Technical College
  Physical Therapist Assistant Prgm.
  92 Western Ave.
  Fairfield, ME 04937-1367
  Tel: 207-453-5147 *Fax:* 207-453-5011
  E-mail: knchandl@kutc.mtcs.tec.me.us

Maryland

Baltimore City Community College
  Physical Therapist Assistant Prgm.
  Nursing Bldg. Rm. 302
  2901 Liberty Heights Ave.
  Baltimore, MD 21215
  Tel: 410-462-7720

Allegany College of Maryland
  Physical Therapist Assistant Prgm.
  12401 Willowbrook Rd. SE
  Cumberland, MD 21502-2596
  Tel: 301-724-7700, ext. 538
  Fax: 301-777-8574
  E-mail: beth@ac.cc.md.us

Montgomery College
  Physical Therapist Assistant Prgm.
  7600 Takoma Ave.
  Takoma Park, MD 20912
  Tel: 301-650-1450 *Fax:* 301-650-1446
  E-mail: jcepeda@mc.cc.md.us

Carroll Community College
  Physical Therapist Assistant Prgm.
  1601 Washington Rd.
  Westminster, MD 21157
  Tel: 410-386-8259, ext. 808
  Fax: 410-876-8855
  E-mail: afrock@carroll.cc.md.us

Massachusetts

Endicott College
  Physical Therapist Assistant Prgm.
  376 Hale St.
  Beverly, MA 01915
  Tel: 508-927-0585, ext. 2310
  Fax: 508-927-6641
  E-mail: jpeters@endicott.edu

Bay State College
  Physical Therapist Assistant Prgm.
  122 Commonwealth Ave.
  Boston, MA 02116
  Tel: 617-236-8000 *Fax:* 617-375-0197

Fisher College
  Physical Therapist Assistant Prgm.
  118 Beacon St.
  Boston, MA 02116
  Tel: 617-236-5457 *Fax:* 617-236-8858

Massasoit Community College
  Physical Therapist Assistant Prgm.
  One Massasoit Blvd.
  Brockton, MA 02402
  Tel: 508-588-9100, ext. 1788
  Fax: 508-588-1250

Newbury College
  Physical Therapist Assistant Prgm.
  129 Fisher Ave.
  Brookline, MA 02146
  Tel: 617-730-7061 *Fax:* 617-730-7182

North Shore Community College
  Physical Therapist Assistant Prgm.
  One Ferncroft Rd.
  Danvers, MA 01923-4093
  Tel: 508-762-4000, ext. 4042
  Fax: 508-762-4022

Mt. Wachusett Community College
  Physical Therapist Assistant Prgm.
  444 Green St.
  Gardner, MA 01440-1000
  Tel: 508-632-6600, ext. 287

Lasell Junior College
  Physical Therapist Assistant Prgm.
  1844 Commonwealth Ave.
  Newton, MA 02166
  Tel: 617-243-2127

Berkshire Community College
  Physical Therapist Assistant Prgm.
  1350 W St.
  Pittsfield, MA 01201-5786
  Tel: 413-499-4660, ext. 313
  Fax: 413-447-7840

Springfield Technical Community
    College
  Physical Therapist Assistant Prgm.
  Bldg. 20/One Armory Sq.
  Springfield, MA 01101
  Tel: 413-781-7822, ext. 3539
  Fax: 413-781-5805

Massachusetts Bay Community
    College
  Physical Therapist Assistant Prgm.
  Wellesley Hills Campus
  50 Oakland St.
  Wellesley Hills, MA 02181-5399
  Tel: 617-239-2500 *Fax:* 617-239-1049

Cape Cod Community College
  Physical Therapist Assistant Prgm.
  2240 Iyanough Rd.
  West Barnstable, MA 02668-1599
  Tel: 508-362-2131, ext. 4335
  Fax: 508-362-3988

Becker College
  Physical Therapist Assistant Prgm.
  61 Sever St.
  Worcester, MA 01615-0071
  Tel: 508-791-9142, ext. 360
  Fax: 508-831-7505

Michigan

Kellogg Community College
  Physical Therapist Assistant Prgm.
  450 North Ave.
  Battle Creek, MI 49017
  Tel: 616-965-3931, ext. 2313
  Fax: 616-965-4133
  E-mail: millerd@kellogg.cc.mi.us

Macomb Community College
  Physical Therapist Assistant Prgm.
  44575 Garfield Rd.
  Clinton Township, MI 48038-1139

Henry Ford Community College
  Physical Therapist Assistant Prgm.
  22586 Ann Arbor Trail
  Dearborn Heights, MI 48127-2598
  Tel: 313-730-5970 *Fax:* 313-359-4601

Mott Community College–Fenton
  Physical Therapist Assistant Prgm.
  Southern Lakes Branch Campus
  2100 W. Thompson Rd.
  Fenton, MI 48430
  Tel: 810-750-8551 *Fax:* 810-750-8588

Baker College
  Physical Therapist Assistant Prgm.
  1050 W. Bristol Rd.
  Flint, MI 48507-5508
  Tel: 810-766-4100 *Fax:* 810-766-4049

Davenport College
Physical Therapist Assistant Prgm.
220 E. Kalamazoo St.
Lansing, MI 48933
Tel: 517-484-2600 *Fax:* 517-484-9719
E-mail: laaperkins@Davenport.edu

Baker College of Muskegon
Physical Therapist Assistant Prgm.
123 Apple Ave.
Muskegon, MI 49442
Tel: 616-726-4904, ext. 341
Fax: 616-726-1417
E-mail: schaub_P@
  muskegon.baker.edu

Delta College
Physical Therapist Assistant Prgm.
F-56 Allied Health Bldg.
University Center, MI 48710
Tel: 517-686-9147 *Fax:* 517-686-8736

Minnesota

Riverland Community College–Albert
  Lea
Physical Therapist Assistant Prgm.
2200 Tech Dr.
Albert Lea, MN 56007-3499
Tel: 507-379-3366 *Fax:* 507-379-3333
E-mail: Admissions:mshepard@
  river.cc.mn.us

Anoka–Hennepin Technical College
Physical Therapist Assistant Prgm.
1355 W. Hwy. 10
Anoka, MN 55303
Tel: 612-576-4700, ext. 4899
Fax: 612-576-4715

Lake Superior College
Physical Therapist Assistant Prgm.
2101 Trinity Rd.
Duluth, MN 55811
Tel: 218-733-7632 *Fax:* 218-723-4921
E-mail: j.worley@lsc.cc.mn.us

Northwest Technical College–East
  Grand Forks
Physical Therapist Assistant Prgm.
Hwy. 220 N
East Grand Forks, MN 56721
Tel: 218-773-3441, ext. 450
Fax: 218-773-4502
E-mail: wilson@mail.ntc.mnslu.edu

College of St. Catherine–Minneapolis
Physical Therapist Assistant Prgm.
601 Twenty-Fifth Ave. S
Minneapolis, MN 55454
Tel: 612-690-7826 *Fax:* 612-690-7849

Mississippi

Itawamba Community College
Physical Therapist Assistant Prgm.
Dept. of Applied Science and
  Technology
602 W. Hill St.
Fulton, MS 38843
Tel: 601-862-3101, ext. 336
Fax: 601-862-9540

Pearl River Community
  College–Hattiesburg
Physical Therapist Assistant Prgm.
5448 U.S. Hwy. 49 S
Hattiesburg, MS 39401
Tel: 601-544-7722 *Fax:* 601-545-2976

Hinds Community College District
Physical Therapist Assistant Prgm.
Nursing Applied Health Center
1750 Chadwick Dr.
Jackson, MS 39204-3490
Tel: 601-371-3512 *Fax:* 601-371-3529

Missouri

Sanford Brown College Hazelwood
  Campus
Physical Therapist Assistant Prgm.
368 Brookes Dr.
Hazelwood, MO 63042
Tel: 314-731-3995 *Fax:* 314-731-7044

Linn State Technical College
Physical Therapist Assistant Prgm.
Capital Region Medical Center
1125 Madison
Jefferson City, MO 65101
Tel: 573-635-7100, ext. 1646

Penn Valley Community College
Physical Therapist Assistant Prgm.
3201 Southwest Trafficway
Kansas City, MO 64111-2764
Tel: 816-759-4241
E-mail: robertsn@pennvalley.cc.mo.us

St. Louis Community College at
  Meramec
  Physical Therapist Assistant Prgm.
  11333 Big Bend Blvd.
  St. Louis, MO 63122
  Tel: 314-984-7385 *Fax:* 314-984-7117

Nebraska

Northeast Community College
  Physical Therapist Assistant Prgm.
  801 E. Benjamin Ave./P.O. Box 469
  Norfolk, NE 68702-0469
  Tel: 402-371-2020 *Fax:* 402-644-0650

Clarkson College
  Physical Therapist Assistant Prgm.
  101 S. Forty-Second St.
  Omaha, NE 68131-2739
  Tel: 402-552-6178 *Fax:* 402-552-6019
  E-mail: peck@clrkcol.crhsnet.edu

Nevada

Community College of Southern
  Nevada
  Physical Therapist Assistant Prgm.
  6375 W. Charleston Blvd.
  Las Vegas, NV 89102
  Tel: 702-651-5588 *Fax:* 702-651-5506

New Hampshire

New Hampshire Community
  Technical College
  Physical Therapist Assistant Prgm.
  One College Dr.
  Claremont, NH 03743-9707
  Tel: 603-542-7744 *Fax:* 603-543-1844

New Jersey

Fairleigh Dickinson University
  Physical Therapist Assistant Prgm.
  285 Madison Ave.
  Madison, NJ 07940
  Tel: 973-443-8746 *Fax:* 973-443-8766

Atlantic Community College
  Physical Therapist Assistant Prgm.
  5100 Black Horse Pike
  Mays Landing, NJ 08330
  Tel: 609-343-5037 *Fax:* 609-343-5122

Essex County College
  Physical Therapist Assistant Prgm.
  303 University Ave.
  Newark, NJ 07102
  Tel: 201-877-3481 *Fax:* 201-623-6449
  E-mail: georgia@essex.edu

Union County College
  Physical Therapist Assistant Prgm.
  Plainfield Campus
  232 E. Second St.
  Plainfield, NJ 07060
  Tel: 908-412-3577 *Fax:* 908-754-2798

New Mexico

San Juan College
  Physical Therapist Assistant Prgm.
  4601 College Blvd.
  Farmington, NM 87402-4699
  Tel: 505-599-0424 *Fax:* 505-599-0385
  E-mail: coppoletti@sjc.cc.nm.us

New York

Maria College
  Physical Therapist Assistant Prgm.
  700 New Scotland Ave.
  Albany, NY 12208-1798
  Tel: 518-489-7436 *Fax:* 518-438-7170

Genesee Community College
  Physical Therapist Assistant Prgm.
  One College Rd.
  Batavia, NY 14020-9704
  Tel: 716-343-6366

Broome Community College
  Physical Therapist Assistant Prgm.
  P.O. Box 1017
  Student Affairs Bldg./Rm. 112
  Binghamton, NY 13902
  Tel: 607-778-5211 *Fax:* 607-778-5345

Nassau Community College
  Physical Therapist Assistant Prgm.
  One Education Dr.
  Garden City, NY 11530
  Tel: 516-572-7550

Herkimer County Community College
  Physical Therapist Assistant Prgm.
  Reservoir Rd.
  Herkimer, NY 13350
  Tel: 315-866-0300, ext. 340
  Fax: 315-866-7523
  E-mail: cedelorme%shccvd@
    itec.suny.edu

LaGuardia Community College
  Physical Therapist Assistant Prgm.
  31-10 Thomson Ave. E 300 K
  Long Island City, NY 11101
  Tel: 718-482-5780 *Fax:* 718-482-5599

Orange County Community College
Physical Therapist Assistant Prgm.
115 South St.
Middletown, NY 10940
Tel: 914-341-4290 *Fax:* 914-343-1228

New York University
Physical Therapist Assistant Prgm.
School of Cont. Educ./11 W. Forty-
    Second St.
Room 518
New York, NY 10036
Tel: 212-790-1633 *Fax:* 212-790-1669

Niagara County Community College
Physical Therapist Assistant Prgm.
Div. of Life Sciences
3111 Saunders Settlement Rd.
Sanborn, NY 14132
Tel: 716-731-3271, ext. 319

Suffolk County Community College
Physical Therapist Assistant Prgm.
Dept. of Health Careers
533 College Rd.
Selden, NY 11784
Tel: 516-451-4299 *Fax:* 516-451-4697

Onondaga Community College
Physical Therapist Assistant Prgm.
Syracuse, NY 13215
Tel: 315-469-2388 *Fax:* 315-469-2593

North Carolina

Stanly Community College
Physical Therapist Assistant Prgm.
141 College Dr.
Albemarle, NC 28001
Tel: 704-982-0121, ext. 226
Fax: 704-982-0819
E-mail: sloanp@aol.com

Central Piedmont Community College
Physical Therapist Assistant Prgm.
P.O. Box 35009
Charlotte, NC 28235
Tel: 704-342-6193 *Fax:* 704-342-5930

Fayetteville Technical Community
    College
Physical Therapist Assistant Prgm.
P.O. Box 35236
Fayetteville, NC 28303
Tel: 910-678-8259 *Fax:* 910-484-6600
E-mail:
    eckele@sunmis2.fagtech.cc.nc.us

Caldwell Community College &
    Technical Institute
Physical Therapist Assistant Prgm.
2855 Hickory Blvd.
Hudson, NC 28638
Tel: 704-726-2457 *Fax:* 704-726-2216

Nash Community College
Physical Therapist Assistant Prgm.
Old Carriage Rd./P.O. Box 7488
Rocky Mount, NC 27804-0488
Tel: 919-443-4011, ext. 281
Fax: 919-443-0828

Southwestern Community College
Physical Therapist Assistant Prgm.
447 College Dr.
Sylva, NC 28789
Tel: 704-586-4091 *Fax:* 704-586-3129
E-mail: debm@southwest.cc.nc.us

Martin Community College
Physical Therapist Assistant Prgm.
1161 Kehukee Park Rd.
Williamston, NC 27892
Tel: 919-792-1521, ext. 265
Fax: 919-792-4425

North Dakota

University of North Dakota–Williston
Physical Therapist Assistant Prgm.
P.O. Box 1326/1410 University Ave.
Williston, ND 58802-1326
Tel: 701-774-4291 *Fax:* 701-774-4275
E-mail: hbenson@basin.und-
    w.hodak.edu

Ohio

Stark State College of Technology
Physical Therapist Assistant Prgm.
Health Technologies Div.
6200 Frank Ave. NW
Canton, OH 44720
Tel: 330-966-5450 *Fax:* 330-966-6586

University of Cincinnati
Physical Therapist Assistant Prgm.
L101 University College/ML 0168
Cincinnati, OH 45221-0168
Tel: 513-556-1726 *Fax:* 513-556-3007

Cuyahoga Community College
Physical Therapist Assistant Prgm.
2900 Community College Ave./S&T
126
Cleveland, OH 44115
Tel: 216-987-4247 *Fax:* 216-987-4386
E-mail: toby.sternheimer@
tri_c.cc.oh.us

Sinclair Community College
Physical Therapist Assistant Prgm.
444 W. Third St.
Dayton, OH 45402
Tel: 513-449-5355 *Fax:* 513-449-5192
E-mail: mkimbro@cleo.sinclair.edu

Kent State University–East Liverpool
Physical Therapist Assistant Prgm.
400 E. Fourth St.
East Liverpool, OH 43920-3497
Tel: 216-385-4272 *Fax:* 216-385-6348

Lima Technical College
Physical Therapist Assistant Prgm.
4240 Campus Dr.
Lima, OH 45804
Tel: 419-221-1112 *Fax:* 419-221-0450

North Central Technical College
Physical Therapist Assistant Prgm.
2441 Kenwood Circle/P.O. Box 698
Mansfield, OH 44901-0698
Tel: 419-755-4773 *Fax:* 419-755-5630

Central Ohio Technical College
Physical Therapist Assistant Prgm.
Dept. of Allied Health and Public
Service
1179 University Dr.
Newark, OH 43055
Tel: 614-366-9360 *Fax:* 614-366-5047

Shawnee State University
Physical Therapist Assistant Prgm.
940 Second St.
Portsmouth, OH 45662
Tel: 614-355-2288 *Fax:* 614-355-2354

Owens Community College
Physical Therapist Assistant Prgm.
P.O. Box 10,000 Oregon Rd.
Toledo, OH 43699-1947
Tel: 419-661-7084 *Fax:* 419-661-7251
E-mail: pbensman@owens.cc.oh.us

Professional Skills Institute
Physical Therapist Assistant Prgm.
20 Arco Dr.
Toledo, OH 43699-1947
Tel: 419-531-9610 *Fax:* 419-531-4732

Oklahoma

SW Oklahoma State University/
Caddo–Kiowa Vocational
Technical Center
Physical Therapist Assistant Prgm.
P.O. Box 190
Ft. Cobb, OK 73038
Tel: 405-643-5511, ext. 262
Fax: 405-643-2144

Oklahoma City Community College
Physical Therapist Assistant Prgm.
7777 S. May Ave.
Oklahoma City, OK 73159
Tel: 405-682-1611, ext. 7305

Carl Albert State College
1507 S. McKenna
Poteau, OK 74953-5208
Tel: 918-647-1350 *Fax:* 918-647-1327

Tulsa Community College
Physical Therapist Assistant Prgm.
909 S. Boston Ave.
Tulsa, OK 74119
Tel: 918-595-7002 *Fax:* 918-595-7091

Oregon

Mt. Hood Community College
Physical Therapist Assistant Prgm.
26000 SE Stark St.
Gresham, OR 97030
Tel: 503-667-7465 *Fax:* 503-492-6047
E-mail: lippertl@mltcc.cc.or.us

Pennsylvania

Harcum College
Physical Therapist Assistant Prgm.
750 Montgomery Ave.
Bryn Mawr, PA 19010
Tel: 610-526-6059 *Fax:* 610-526-6031

Butler County Community College
Physical Therapist Assistant Prgm.
P.O. Box 1203
Butler, PA 16003-1203
Tel: 412-287-8711, ext. 372
Fax: 412-285-6047

Mt. Aloysius College
Physical Therapist Assistant Prgm.
7373 Admiral Peary Hwy.
Cresson, PA 16630
Tel: 814-886-6355 *Fax:* 814-886-2978

Penn State University–DuBois
Physical Therapist Assistant Prgm.
College Pl.
DuBois, PA 15801
Tel: 814-375-4700

Mercyhurst College
Physical Therapist Assistant Prgm.
Glenwood Hills
501 E. Thirty-Eighth St./Box 411
Erie, PA 16546-0001
Tel: 814-824-2083 *Fax:* 814-824-3101
E-mail: qlqz@prodigy.com

Penn State University–Hazelton
Physical Therapist Assistant Prgm.
Box 704-A
Hazelton, PA 18201
Tel: 717-450-3047 *Fax:* 717-450-3182

Keystone College
Physical Therapist Assistant Prgm.
Allied Health and Environmental Sci.
   Div.
P.O. Box 50
La Plume, PA 18440-0200
Tel: 800-824-2764 *Fax:* 717-945-6770

Community College of Allegheny
   County
Physical Therapist Assistant Prgm.
595 Beatty Rd.
Monroeville, PA 15146
Tel: 412-325-6663

Penn State University–Mont Alto
Physical Therapist Assistant Prgm.
Campus Dr.
Mont Alto, PA 17237-9703
Tel: 717-749-6217 *Fax:* 717-749-6069

Allegheny University of the Health
   Sciences
Physical Therapist Assistant Prgm.
Broad and Vine Sts./MS525
Philadelphia, PA 19102-1192
Tel: 215-762-4818 *Fax:* 215-246-5347

Alvernia College
Physical Therapist Assistant Prgm.
400 Bernadine St.
Reading, PA 19607
Tel: 610-796-8226 *Fax:* 610-796-8349

Lehigh Carbon Community College
Physical Therapist Assistant Prgm.
4525 Education Park Dr.
Schnecksville, PA 18078-2598
Tel: 610-799-1556 *Fax:* 610-799-1527

Penn State University–Shenango
Physical Therapist Assistant Prgm.
147 Shenango Ave.
Sharon, PA 16146
Tel: 412-983-2814 *Fax:* 412-983-9863

Central Pennsylvania Business School
Physical Therapist Assistant Prgm.
Campus on College Hill
Summerdale, PA 17093-0309
Tel: 717-732-0702, ext. 2231
Fax: 717-732-5254

Puerto Rico

Humacao University College
Physical Therapist Assistant Prgm.
CUH Postal Station
Humacao, PR 00791
Tel: 787-850-9390 *Fax:* 787-850-9461

Ponce Technological University
   College
Physical Therapist Assistant Prgm.
University of Puerto Rico Regl. Coll.
   Admin.
P.O. Box 7186
Ponce, PR 00732
Tel: 787-844-8181, ext. 246
Fax: 787-844-8108

Rhode Island

Community College of Rhode Island
Physical Therapist Assistant Prgm.
275 Broadway
Newport, RI 02840-2612
Tel: 401-847-9800 *Fax:* 401-846-9051

South Carolina

Trident Technical College
Physical Therapist Assistant Prgm.
P.O. Box 118067 AH-M
Charleston, SC 29423-8067
Tel: 803-574-6141 *Fax:* 803-574-6585

Greenville Technical College
Physical Therapist Assistant Prgm.
P.O. Box 5616
Greenville, SC 29606-5616
Tel: 864-848-2037 *Fax:* 864-250-8462

South Dakota

Lake Area Technical Institute
Physical Therapist Assitant Prgm.
230 Eleventh St. NE/P.O. Box 730
Watertown, SD 57201-0730
Tel: 605-886-5284 *Fax:* 605-886-6299

Tennessee

Chattanooga State Technical
  Community College
Physical Therapist Assistant Prgm.
4501 Amnicola Hwy.
Chattanooga, TN 37406-1097
Tel: 423-697-4450 *Fax:* 423-634-3071

Volunteer State Community College
Physical Therapist Assistant Prgm.
1480 Nashville Pike
Gallatin, TN 37066
Tel: 615-452-8600, ext. 3336
Fax: 615-452-3224

Jackson State Community College
Physical Therapist Assistant Prgm.
2046 N. Parkway St.
Jackson, TN 38301-3797
Tel: 901-425-2612 *Fax:* 901-425-2647

Shelby State Community College
Physical Therapist Assistant Prgm.
P.O. Box 40568
Memphis, TN 38174-0568
Tel: 901-544-5394 *Fax:* 901-544-5391

Walters State Community College
Physical Therapist Assistant Prgm.
500 S. Davy Crockett Pkwy.
Morristown, TN 37813-6899
Tel: 423-585-6982 *Fax:* 423-585-6870

Roane State Community College
Physical Therapist Assistant Prgm.
728 Emory Valley Rd.
Oak Ridge, TN 37830
Tel: 423-481-3496 *Fax:* 423-483-0447

Texas

Amarillo College
Physical Therapist Assistant Prgm.
P.O. Box 447
Amarillo, TX 79178
Tel: 806-354-6043 *Fax:* 806-354-6076

Austin Community College
Physical Therapist Assistant Prgm.
Riverside Campus
1020 Grove Blvd.
Austin, TX 78741
Tel: 512-283-6189 *Fax:* 512-385-9683

El Paso Community College
Physical Therapist Assistant Prgm.
Rio Grande Campus/P.O. Box 20500
El Paso, TX 79998
Tel: 915-534-4172 *Fax:* 915-534-4114

Houston Community College System
Physical Therapist Assistant Prgm.
3100 Shenandoah
Houston, TX 77021-1098
Tel: 713-718-7381 *Fax:* 713-718-7401

Tarrant Junior College
Physical Therapist Assistant Prgm.
828 Harwood Rd./Northeast Campus
Hurst, TX 76054
Tel: 817-788-6435 *Fax:* 817-788-6601

Kilgore College
Physical Therapist Assistant Prgm.
1100 Broadway
Kilgore, TX 75662
Tel: 903-983-8146 *Fax:* 903-983-8600

Laredo Community College
Physical Therapist Assistant Prgm.
West End Washington St.
Campus Box 153
Laredo, TX 78040
Tel: 210-721-5263 *Fax:* 210-721-5431
E-mail: apuig@icsi.net

Odessa College
Physical Therapist Assistant Prgm.
201 W. University Blvd.
Odessa, TX 79764
Tel: 915-335-6842 *Fax:* 915-335-6846

St. Philip's College
Physical Therapist Assistant Prgm.
1801 Martin Luther King Dr.
San Antonio, TX 78203-2098
Tel: 512-531-3416 *Fax:* 512-531-4811

Community College of the Air Force
Physical Therapist Assistant Prgm.
382 MTS
917 Missile Rd./Ste. 3
Sheppard AFB, TX 76311-2263
Tel: 817-676-3873 *Fax:* 817-676-3850
E-mail: beandryl@spd.aetc.at.mil

McLennan Community College
Physical Therapist Assistant Prgm.
1400 College Dr.
Waco, TX 76708
Tel: 254-299-8825 *Fax:* 254-299-8435
E-mail: bbg@mcc.cc.tx.us

Wharton County Junior College
Physical Therapist Assistant Prgm.
911 Boling Hwy.
Wharton, TX 77488
Tel: 409-532-6393 *Fax:* 409-532-6489

Utah

Salt Lake Community College
Physical Therapist Assistant Prgm.
P.O. Box 30808
4600 S. Redwood Rd.
Salt Lake City, UT 84130-0808
Tel: 801-957-4054 *Fax:* 801-957-5708
E-mail: ploegedi@slcc.edu

Virginia

Northern Virginia Community College
Physical Therapist Assistant Prgm.
8333 Little River Trnpk.
Annandale, VA 22003
Tel: 703-323-3386 *Fax:* 703-323-4576

John Tyler Community College
Physical Therapist Assistant Prgm.
13101 Jefferson Davis Hwy.
Chester, VA 23831
Tel: 804-796-4040 *Fax:* 804-796-4359
E-mail: jtbowmd@jt.cc.va.us

College of Health Sciences
Physical Therapist Assistant Prgm.
Coll. of Health Sciences
P.O. Box 13186/920 S. Jefferson St.
Roanoke, VA 24031-3186
Tel: 540-985-8398 *Fax:* 540-985-9773

Tidewater Community College
Physical Therapist Assistant Prgm.
1700 College Crescent/Bldg. E/Rm.
E101
Virginia Beach, VA 23456-1918
Tel: 757-822-7301 *Fax:* 757-427-1338

Wytheville Community College
Physical Therapist Assistant Prgm.
1000 E. Main St.
Wytheville, VA 24382
Tel: 540-223-4717 *Fax:* 540-223-4778

Washington

Green River Community College
Physical Therapist Assistant Prgm.
Health Sciences Div./Mailstop OE-14
12401 SE 320th St.
Auburn, WA 98002-3699
Tel: 253-833-9111, ext. 4343
E-mail: bbrucker@qrcc.ctc.edu

Whatcom Community College
Physical Therapist Assistant Prgm.
237 W. Kellog Rd.
Bellingham, WA 98226
Tel: 360-676-2170 *Fax:* 360-676-2171
E-mail: bgraves@whatcom.ctc.edu

Wisconsin

Northeast Wisconsin Technical College
Physical Therapist Assistant Prgm.
2740 W. Mason St.
Green Bay, WI 54307
Tel: 920-498-5543 *Fax:* 920-498-5673

Blackhawk Technical College
Physical Therapist Assistant Prgm.
6004 Prairie Rd./County Trunk G
Janesville, WI 53547-5009
Tel: 608-757-7632

Western Wisconsin Technical College
Physical Therapist Assistant Prgm.
304 N. Sixth St.
LaCrosse, WI 54602-0908
Tel: 608-785-9702 *Fax:* 608 785-9407
E-mail: herlitzke@al.western.tec.wi.us

Milwaukee Area Technical College
Physical Therapist Assistant Prgm.
Health Occupations Div.
700 W. State St.
Milwaukee, WI 53233
Tel: 414-297-7148 *Fax:* 414-297-6851

OCCUPATIONAL THERAPY ASSISTANT TRAINING PROGRAMS

Alabama

Jefferson State Community College
Occupational Therapy Asst. Prgm.
Pinson Valley Pkwy.
2601 Carson Rd.
Birmingham, AL 35215-3098
Tel: 205-856-6043 *Fax:* 205-856-7725
E-mail: health@jscc.al.us

Wallace State College
Occupational Therapy Asst. Prgm.
P.O. Box 2000
Hanceville, AL 35077-2000
Tel: 205-352-8333 *Fax:* 205-352-8320
E-mail: hazard@bham.mindspring.com

Arizona

Apollo College
Occupational Therapy Asst. Prgm.
2701 W. Bethany Home Rd.
Phoenix, AZ 85017-1705
Tel: 602-433-1333 *Fax:* 602-433-1414

California

Grossmont College
Occupational Therapy Asst. Prgm.
8800 Grossmont College Dr.
El Cajon, CA 92020-1799
Tel: 619-644-7305 *Fax:* 619-644-7961

Fresno City College
Occupational Therapy Asst. Prgm.
Loma Linda University
SAHP–Nichol Hall Rm. A912
Loma Linda, CA 92350-0001
Tel: 909-824-4628 *Fax:* 909-478-4239
E-mail: lhewitt@sahp.llu.edu

Loma Linda University
Occupational Therapy Asst. Prgm.
Sch. of Allied Hlth. Professions
SAHP–Nichol Hall/Rm. A912
Loma Linda, CA 92350–0001
Tel: 909-824-4948 *Fax:* 909-824-4791
E-mail: lhewitt@sahp.llu.edu

Mt. St. Mary's College
Occupational Therapy Asst. Prgm.
Doheny Campus
10 Chester Pl.
Los Angeles, CA 90007-2598
Tel: 213-477-2581 *Fax:* 213-477-2519
E-mail: esiegmund@msmc.la.edu

Western Institute of Science & Health
Occupational Therapy Asst. Prgm.
120 Avram Ave.
Rohnert Park, CA 94928
Tel: 707-664-9267 *Fax:* 707-664-9237
E-mail: wish@sonic.net

Sacramento City College
Occupational Therapy Asst. Prgm.
Allied Health Dept.
3835 Freeport Blvd.
Sacramento, CA 95822
Tel: 916-558-2297 *Fax:* 916-558-2392

Maric College of Medical Careers
Occupational Therapy Asst. Prgm.
3666 Kearny Villa Rd.
San Diego, CA 92123
Tel: 619-654-3650 *Fax:* 619-279-1620

Colorado

Denver Institute of Technology
Occupational Therapy Asst. Prgm.
Health Careers Div.
7350 N. Broadway
Denver, CO 80221
Tel: 303-650-5050 *Fax:* 303-657-5529
E-mail: kmcbride@dit.tec.co.us

Denver Technical College
Occupational Therapy Asst. Prgm.
925 S. Niagara St.
Denver, CO 80224-1658
Tel: 303-329-3340, ext. 295
Fax: 303-321-5820
E-mail: asolomon@dtc.edu

Morgan Community College
Occupational Therapy Asst. Prgm.
17800 Rd. 20
Ft. Morgan, CA 80701-4399
Tel: 970-867-3081 *Fax:* 970-867-6608
E-mail:
s_zapiecki%mcc@cccs.cccoes.edu

Arapahoe Community College
Occupational Therapy Asst. Prgm.
2500 W. College Dr./P.O. Box 9002
Littleton, CO 80160-9002
Tel: 303-797-5939 *Fax:* 303-797-5935

Pueblo Community College
Occupational Therapy Asst. Prgm.
900 W. Orman Ave.
Pueblo, CO 81004-1499
Tel: 719-549-3268 *Fax:* 719-549-3136
E-mail: hawkins@pcc.cccoes.edu

Connecticut

Manchester Community–Technical
College
Occupational Therapy Asst. Prgm.
60 Bidwell St. MS 19 P.O. Box 1046
Manchester, CT 06040-1046
Tel: 860-647-6183
E-mail: ma_smaga@comnet.edu

Briarwood College
Occupational Therapy Asst. Prgm.
2279 Mount Vernon Rd.
Southington, CT 06489
Tel: 860-628-4751 *Fax:* 860-628-6444

Delaware

Delaware Technical and Community
College–Owens Campus
Occupational Therapy Asst. Prgm.
Owens Campus/P.O. Box 610
Georgetown, DE 19947-0610
Tel: 302-856-5400 *Fax:* 302-856-5773
E-mail: alawton@outland.dtcc.edu

Florida

Daytona Beach Community College
Occupational Therapy Asst. Prgm.
1200 International Speedway Blvd.
Daytona Beach, FL 32114
Tel: 904-255-8131 *Fax:* 904-254-4491

Palm Beach Community College
Occupational Therapy Asst. Prgm.
4200 S. Congress Ave.
Lake Worth, FL 33461-4796
Tel: 561-439-8094 *Fax:* 561-439-8202

Central Florida Community College
Occupational Therapy Asst. Prgm.
3001 SW College Rd.
Ocala, FL 34474
Tel: 352-237-2111, ext. 327
E-mail: hypw87a@prodigy

Hillsborough Community College
Occupational Therapy Asst. Prgm.
P.O. Box 30030
Tampa, FL 33630-3030
Tel: 813-253-7431 *Fax:* 813-253-7506

Georgia

Medical College of Georgia
Occupational Therapy Asst. Prgm.
EF 102
Augusta, GA 30912-0700
Tel: 706-721-3641 *Fax:* 706-721-9718
E-mail: rcarrasc@mail.mcg.edu

Middle Georgia College
Occupational Therapy Asst. Prgm.
1100 Second St. SE
Cochran, GA 31014-1599
Tel: 912-934-3402 *Fax:* 912-934-3461
E-mail:
    hcopan@warrior.mgc.peachnet.edu

Hawaii

Kapiolani Community College
Occupational Therapy Asst. Prgm.
Health Sciences Dept.
4303 Diamond Head Rd./Kavila 210
Honolulu, HI 96816
Tel: 808-734-9229

Idaho

American Institute of Health
Technology
Occupational Therapy Asst. Prgm.
6600 Emerald
Boise, ID 83704-8738
Tel: 208-377-8080 *Fax:* 208-322-7658
E-mail: moric@micron.net

Illinois

Parkland College
Occupational Therapy Asst. Prgm.
2400 W. Bradley Ave.
Champaign, IL 61821-1899
Tel: 217-351-2394 *Fax:* 217-373-3830
E-mail: rbahnke@parkland.cc.il.usa

Wilbur Wright College
Occupational Therapy Asst. Prgm.
4300 N. Narragansett Ave.
Chicago, IL 60634
Tel: 773-481-8875 *Fax:* 773-481-8892
E-mail: jwandel@ccc.edu

College of DuPage
Occupational Therapy Asst. Prgm.
Occupational and Vocational Education
425 Twenty-Second St.
Glen Ellyn, IL 60137-6599
Tel: 630-942-2419 *Fax:* 630-858-5409

Southern Illinois Collegiate Common Mkt.
Occupational Therapy Asst. Prgm.
3213 S. Park Ave.
Herrin, IL 62948
Tel: 618-942-6902 *Fax:* 618-942-6658
E-mail: siccm@midwest.net

Illinois Central College
Occupational Therapy Asst. Prgm.
201 SW Adams St.
Peoria, IL 61635-0001
Tel: 309-999-4674 *Fax:* 309-673-9626

South Suburban College of Cook County
Occupational Therapy Asst. Prgm.
15800 S. State St.
South Holland, IL 60473-1262
Tel: 708-596-2000, ext. 264
Fax: 708-210-5758
E-mail: ssclib@cedar.cic.net

Indiana

Ivy Technical State College–Indianapolis
Occupational Therapy Asst. Prgm.
Central Indiana Region
One W. Twenty-Sixth St./P.O. Box 1763
Indianapolis, IN 46206-1763
Tel: 317-921-4325 *Fax:* 317-921-4511
E-mail: ctroxell@ivy.tec.in.us

Iowa

Kirkwood Community College
Occupational Therapy Asst. Prgm.
6301 Kirkwood Blvd., SW/P.O. Box 2068
Cedar Rapids, IA 52406-9973
Tel: 319-398-4941 *Fax:* 319-398-1293
E-mail: mdunfor@kirkwood.cc.ia.us

Western Iowa Technical Community College
Occupational Therapy Asst. Prgm.
4647 Stone Ave./P.O. Box 265
Sioux City, IA 51102-0265
Tel: 712-274-8733 *Fax:* 712-274-6412

Kansas

Barton County Community College
Occupational Therapy Asst. Prgm.
R.R. 3 Box 136Z
Great Bend, KS 67530-9283
Tel: 316-792-9368 *Fax:* 316-786-1163
E-mail: fryel@cougar.barton.cc.ks.us

Kentucky

Kentucky Tech–Madisonville Health Technical Center
Occupational Therapy Asst. Prgm.
750 N. Laffoon St.
Madisonville, KY 42431
Tel: 502-824-7552 *Fax:* 502-824-7069

Louisiana

Northeast Louisiana University
Occupational Therapy Asst. Prgm.
Coll. of Pharmacy and Hlth. Sci.
Sch. Allied Hlth. Sciences
Monroe, LA 71209-0430
Tel: 318-342-1610 *Fax:* 318-342-5584
E-mail: ALDAVIS@alpha.nlu.edu

Delgado Community College
Occupational Therapy Asst. Prgm.
City Park Campus
615 City Park Ave.
New Orleans, LA 70119
Tel: 504-483-4980 *Fax:* 504-483-4609
E-mail: lkelly@pop3.dcc.edu

Maine

Kennebec Valley Technical College
Occupational Therapy Asst. Prgm.
92 Western Ave.
Fairfield, ME 04937-1367
Tel: 207-453-5172 *Fax:* 207-453-5010
E-mail: kdsauter@kvtc.mtcs.tec.me.us

Maryland

Catonsville Community College
Occupational Therapy Asst. Prgm.
800 S. Rolling Rd.
Baltimore, MD 21228-9987
Tel: 410-455-4482 *Fax:* 410-719-6501

Allegheny College of Maryland
Occupational Therapy Asst. Prgm.
12401 Willowbrook Rd. SE
Cumberland, MD 21502-2596
Tel: 301-724-7700, ext. 536

Massachusetts

Lasell Junior College
Occupational Therapy Asst. Prgm.
1844 Commonwealth Ave.
Auburndale, MA 02166
Tel: 617-243-2172 *Fax:* 617-243-2326

Bay State College
Occupational Therapy Asst. Prgm.
31 St. James Ave.
Boston, MA 02116
Tel: 617-375-0195 *Fax:* 617-375-0197

North Shore Community College
Occupational Therapy Asst. Prgm.
One Ferncroft Rd./P.O. Box 3340
Danvers, MA 01923-0840
Tel: 508-762-4176 *Fax:* 508-762-4022
E-mail: mnardell@nscc.mass.edu

Bristol Community College
Occupational Therapy Asst. Prgm.
777 Elsbree St.
Fall River, MA 02720-9960
Tel: 508-678-2811, ext. 2325
Fax: 508-676-7146
E-mail: jduponte@bristol.mass.edu

Greenfield Community College
Occupational Therapy Asst. Prgm.
270 Main St.
Greenfield, MA 01301
Tel: 413-774-3131, ext. 316
Fax: 413-774-2285
E-mail: nursing@gcc.mass.edu

Bay Path College
Occupational Therapy Asst. Prgm.
588 Longmeadow St.
Longmeadow, MA 01106
Tel: 413-567-0621 *Fax:* 413-567-9324

Mt. Ida College
Occupational Therapy Asst. Prgm.
Junior College Div./777 Dedham St.
Newton Centre, MA 02159-3310
Tel: 617-928-4770 *Fax:* 617-244-7532
E-mail: jerrie@aol.com

Springfield Technical Community
    College
Occupational Therapy Asst. Prgm.
One Armory Square
Springfield, MA 01101
Tel: 413-781-7822

Massachusetts Bay Community College
Occupational Therapy Asst. Prgm.
Wellesley Hills Campus
50 Oakland St.
Wellesley Hills, MA 02181-5399
Tel: 617-239-2240 *Fax:* 617-239-1047
E-mail: leigh@mbcc.mass.edu

Becker College
Occupational Therapy Asst. Prgm.
61 Sever St., Box 15071
Worcester, MA 01615-0071
Tel: 508-791-9241 *Fax:* 508-831-7505

Quinsigamond Community College
Occupational Therapy Asst. Prgm.
670 W. Boylston St.
Worcester, MA 01606
Tel: 508-853-2300 *Fax:* 508-852-6943

Michigan

Macomb Community College
Occupational Therapy Asst. Prgm.
44575 Garfield Rd.
Clinton Township, MI 48038-1139
Tel: 810-286-2188 *Fax:* 810-286-2098
E-mail: jpacker@macomb.cc.mi.us

Wayne County Community College
Occupational Therapy Asst. Prgm.
801 W. Fort St.
Detroit, MI 48226-9975
Tel: 313-496-2692

Charles Stewart Mott Community
    College
Occupational Therapy Asst. Prgm.
Southern Lakes Campus
2100 W. Thompson Rd.
Fenton, MI 48430
Tel: 810-750-8550 *Fax:* 810-750-8588

Schoolcraft College
Occupational Therapy Asst. Prgm.
1751 Radcliff St.
Garden City, MI 48135-1197
Tel: 313-462-4770, ext. 6002
Fax: 313-462-4775

Grand Rapids Community College
Occupational Therapy Asst. Prgm.
143 Bostwick, NE
Grand Rapids, MI 49503-3295
Tel: 616-771-4236 *Fax:* 616-771-4005
E-mail: adonahue@post.grcc.cc.mi.us

Baker College of Muskegon
Occupational Therapy Asst. Prgm.
1903 Marquette
Muskegon, MI 49442
Tel: 616-777-8800, ext. 5274
Fax: 515-777-5291
E-mail:
  boynto_s@muskegon.baker.edu

Lake Michigan College
Occupational Therapy Asst. Prgm.
South Campus/111 Spruce St.
Niles, MI 49120
Tel: 616-684-5850 *Fax:* 616-684-3270
E-mail: branson@raptor.lmc.cc.mi.us

Minnesota

Anoka–Hennepin Technical College
Occupational Therapy Asst. Prgm.
1355 W. Highway 10
Anoka, MN 55303-1590
Tel: 612-576-4935 *Fax:* 612-576-4715
E-mail: msaxon@ank.tec.mn.us

Riverland Community College
Occupational Therapy Asst. Prgm.
1900 Eighth Ave., NW
Austin, MN 55912-1407
Tel: 507-433-0567 *Fax:* 507-433-0515
E-mail: Davisca@au.cc.mn.us

Lake Superior College
Occupational Therapy Asst. Prgm.
2101 Trinity Rd.
Duluth, MN 55811-3399
Tel: 218-733-7682, ext. 332
Fax: 218-723-4921
E-mail: jdreher@lsc.cc.mn.us

Northwest Technical College–East
  Grand Forks
Occupational Therapy Asst. Prgm.
Hwy. 220 N.
E. Grand Forks, MN 56721
Tel: 218-773-3441 *Fax:* 218-773-4502
E-mail: hilts@adm.egf.tec.mn.us

College of St. Catherine–Minneapolis
Occupational Therapy Asst. Prgm.
601 Twenty-Fifth Ave. S
Minneapolis, MN 55454-1494
Tel: 612-690-7772 *Fax:* 612-690-7849
E-mail: mfchristians@alex.state.edu

Mississippi

Pearl River Community
  College–Hattiesburg
Occupational Therapy Asst. Prgm.
5448 U.S. Hwy. 49 S
Hattiesburg, MS 39401
Tel: 601-554-9141 *Fax:* 601-554-9148

Missouri

Sanford Brown College Hazelwood
  Campus
Occupational Therapy Asst. Prgm.
Hazelwood Campus
368 Brookes Dr.
Hazelwood, MO 63042
Tel: 314-731-3995 *Fax:* 314-731-7044

Penn Valley Community College
Occupational Therapy Asst. Prgm.
3201 SW Trafficway
Kansas City, MO 64111-2764
Tel: 816-759-4235 *Fax:* 816-759-4553
E-mail: mcilnay@pennvalley.cc.mo.us

Rolla Technical Institute
Occupational Therapy Asst. Prgm.
St. Louis Community College at
  Maramec
11333 Big Bend Blvd.
St. Louis, MO 63122
Tel: 314-984-7364 *Fax:* 314-984-7250

St. Louis Community College at
  Meramec
Occupational Therapy Asst. Prgm.
11333 Big Bend Blvd.
St. Louis, MO 63122
Tel: 314-984-7364 *Fax:* 314-984-7250

Montana

Montana State University College of
  Technology
Occupational Therapy Asst. Prgm.
Allied Health Dept./2100 Sixteenth
  Ave. S
Great Falls, MT 59405-4998
Tel: 406-771-4364 *Fax:* 406-771-4317
E-mail: zgf6018@
  maia.oscs.montana.edu

Nebraska

Clarkson College
  Occupational Therapy Asst. Prgm.
  101 S. Forty-Second St.
  Omaha, NE 68131-2739
  Tel: 402-552-6139 *Fax:* 402-552-6019
  E-mail: parde@clrkcol.crhsnet.edu

Nevada

Community College of Southern
    Nevada
  Occupational Therapy Asst. Prgm.
  6375 W. Charleston Blvd.—900
  Las Vegas, NV 89102-1124
  Tel: 702-651-5581 *Fax:* 702-651-5506
  E-mail: presson@ccsn.nevada.edu

New Hampshire

New Hampshire Community
    Technical College
  Occupational Therapy Asst. Prgm.
  One College Dr.
  Claremont, NH 03743-9707
  Tel: 603-542-7744 *Fax:* 603-542-1844
  E-mail: j_larsen@pste.tec.nh.us

New Jersey

Atlantic Community College
  Occupational Therapy Asst. Prgm.
  Allied Health Division
  5100 Black Horse Pike
  Mays Landing, NJ 08330-9888
  Tel: 609-343-5044 *Fax:* 609-343-5122
  E-mail: busillo@nsvm.atlantic.edu

Union County College
  Occupational Therapy Asst. Prgm.
  232 E. Second St.
  Plainfield, NJ 07060
  Tel: 908-412-3587 *Fax:* 908-754-2798
  E-mail: keating@hawk.ucc.edu

New Mexico

Eastern New Mexico
    University–Roswell
  Occupational Therapy Asst. Prgm.
  Div. of Health
  52 Univ. Blvd./P.O. Box 6000
  Roswell, NM 88202-6000
  Tel: 505-624-7267 *Fax:* 505-624-7100
  E-mail:
    herrerap@lib.enmuros.cc.nm.us

Western New Mexico University
  Occupational Therapy Asst. Prgm.
  P.O. Box 680
  Silver City, NM 88062-0680
  Tel: 505-538-6293 *Fax:* 505-538-6178

New York

Maria College
  Occupational Therapy Asst. Prgm.
  700 New Scotland Ave.
  Albany, NY 12208-1798
  Tel: 518-489-7436 *Fax:* 518-438-7170

Genesee Community College
  Occupational Therapy Asst. Prgm.
  One College Rd.
  Batavia, NY 14020-9704
  Tel: 716-343-0055, ext. 6838
  Fax: 716-343-0433

Suffolk County Community College
  Occupational Therapy Asst. Prgm.
  Western Campus
  Crooked Hill Road
  Brentwood, NY 11717-1092
  Tel: 516-851-6752 *Fax:* 516-851-6532

Erie Community College–City Campus
  Occupational Therapy Asst. Prgm.
  6205 Main St.
  Williamsville, NY 14221-7095
  Tel: 716-851-1320 *Fax:* 716-851-1429

Herkimer County Community College
  Occupational Therapy Asst. Prgm.
  Reservoir Rd.
  Herkimer, NY 13350-1598
  Tel: 315-866-0300, ext. 237
  Fax: 315-866-7253

LaGuardia Community College
  Occupational Therapy Asst. Prgm.
  31-10 Thomson Ave.
  Long Island City, NY 11101-3083
  Tel: 718-482-5776

Orange County Community College
  Occupational Therapy Asst. Prgm.
  115 South St.
  Middletown, NY 10940-6404
  Tel: 914-341-4323 *Fax:* 914-343-1228
  E-mail: msands@mail.sunyorange.edu

Rockland Community College
Occupational Therapy Asst. Prgm.
145 College Rd.
Suffern, NY 10901-3699
Tel: 914-574-4312

North Carolina

Stanly Community College
Occupational Therapy Asst. Prgm.
141 College Dr.
Albemarle, NC 28001-9402
Tel: 704-982-0121, ext. 209
Fax: 704-982-0819
E-mail: Babcocks@Stanly.cc.nc.us

Durham Technical Community College
Occupational Therapy Asst. Prgm.
1637 Lawson St.
Durham, NC 27703-5023
Tel: 919-686-3459 *Fax:* 919-686-3601
E-mail: teepas@nando.net

Pitt Community College
Occupational Therapy Asst. Prgm.
P.O. Drawer 7007/Highway 11 S
Greenville, NC 27835-7007
Tel: 919-321-4458 *Fax:* 919-321-4451
E-mail: rarmstro@pcc.pitt.cc.nc.us

Caldwell Community College and
    Technical Institute
Occupational Therapy Asst. Prgm.
2855 Hickory Blvd.
Hudson, NC 28638-1399
Tel: 704-726-2354 *Fax:* 704-726-2216

Southwestern Community College
Occupational Therapy Asst. Prgm.
447 College Dr.
Sylva, NC 28779
Tel: 704-586-4091, ext. 272
Fax: 704-586-3129
E-mail: helenn@southwest.cc.nc.us

North Dakota

North Dakota State College of Science
Occupational Therapy Asst. Prgm.
Hektner Hall
Wahpeton, ND 58076-0002
Tel: 701-671-2982 *Fax:* 701-671-2587
E-mail: mauer@plains.nodak.edu

Ohio

Stark Technical College
Occupational Therapy Asst. Prgm.
6200 Frank Ave., NW
Canton, OH 44720-7299
Tel: 330-966-5458, ext. 200
Fax: 330-966-6586
E-mail: dhuston@stark.cc.oh.us

Cincinnati State Technical and
    Community College
Occupational Therapy Asst. Prgm.
3520 Central Pkwy.
Cincinnati, OH 45223
Tel: 513-569-1598 *Fax:* 513-569-1659
E-mail: ZobayA@cinstate.cc.oh.us

Cuyahoga Community College
Occupational Therapy Asst. Prgm.
2900 Community College Ave.
Cleveland, OH 44115-3196
Tel: 216-987-4498 *Fax:* 216-987-4386

Sinclair Community College
Occupational Therapy Asst. Prgm.
444 W. Third St.
Dayton, OH 45402-1460
Tel: 513-449-5178 *Fax:* 513-449-5175
E-mail: kashwort@sinclair.edu

Kent State University
Occupational Therapy Asst. Prgm.
East Liverpool Campus/400 E. Fourth
    St.
East Liverpool, OH 43920-3497
Tel: 330-385-4272 *Fax:* 330-385-6348

Shawnee State University
Occupational Therapy Asst. Prgm.
Dept. of Occupational Therapy
940 Second St.
Portsmouth, OH 45662-4303
Tel: 614-355-2272 *Fax:* 614-355-2354
E-mail: cperry@shawnee.edu

Lourdes College
Occupational Therapy Asst. Prgm.
6832 Convent Blvd.
Sylvania, OH 43560-2898
Tel: 419-885-3211 *Fax:* 419-882-3786

Muskingum Area Technical College
Occupational Therapy Asst. Prgm.
1555 Newark Rd.
Zanesville, OH 43701-2694
Tel: 614-454-2501 *Fax:* 614-454-0035
E-mail: (marnold@mate.tec.oh.us)

Oklahoma

SW Oklahoma State University/
  Caddo–Kiowa Vocational
  Technical Center
Occupational Therapy Asst. Prgm.
P.O. Box 190
Fort Cobb, OK 73038
Tel: 405-643-5511 *Fax:* 405-643-2144

Oklahoma City Community College
Occupational Therapy Asst. Prgm.
Hlth., Soc. Sci., and Human Svcs. Div.
7777 S. May Ave.
Oklahoma City, OK 73159-4444
Tel: 405-682-7506 *Fax:* 405-682-1611
E-mail: phbaker@okc.cc.ok.us

Tulsa Community College
Occupational Therapy Asst. Prgm.
Allied Hlth. Serv. Division
909 S. Boston Ave.
Tulsa, OK 74119-2095
Tel: 918-595-7319

Oregon

Mt. Hood Community College
Occupational Therapy Asst. Prgm.
26000 SE Stark St.
Gresham, OR 97030-3300
Tel: 503-667-7129 *Fax:* 503-492-6047
E-mail: hencins@mhcc.cc.or.us

Pennsylvania

Harcum College
Occupational Therapy Asst. Prgm.
Bryn Mawr, PA 19010-3476
Tel: 610-526-6115 *Fax:* 610-526-6031

Mt. Aloysius College
Occupational Therapy Asst. Prgm.
Cresson, PA 16630
Tel: 814-886-6328

Penn State University–DuBois
Occupational Therapy Asst. Program
College Place
Dubois, PA 15801-3199
Tel: 814-375-4748 *Fax:* 814-375-4784

Penn State University
Occupational Therapy Asst. Prgm.
Worthington Scranton Campus
120 Ridge View Dr.
Dunmore, PA 18512-1699
Tel: 717-963-4766 *Fax:* 727-963-4783

Community College of Allegheny
  County
Occupational Therapy Asst. Prgm.
595 Beatty Rd.
Monroeville, PA 15146-1395
Tel: 412-325-6751 *Fax:* 412-325-6799
E-mail: lbriola@ccac.edu

Penn State University
Occupational Therapy Asst. Prgm.
Mont Alto Campus
Campus Dr.
Mont Alto, PA 17237-9703
Tel: 717-749-6218
E-mail: jud102@psu.edu

Clarion University of
  Pennsylvania–Venango Campus
Occupational Therapy Asst. Prgm.
1801 W. First St.
Oil City, PA 16301
Tel: 814-676-6591, ext. 241
Fax: 814-676-1348
E-mail: jhatton@mail.clarion.edu

Lehigh Carbon Community College
Occupational Therapy Asst. Prgm.
4525 Education Park Dr.
Schnecksville, PA 18078-2598
Tel: 610-799-1548 *Fax:* 616-799-1527

Penn State University–Shenango
Occupational Therapy Asst. Prgm.
147 Shenango Ave.
Sharon, PA 16146-1537
Tel: 412-983-2867 *Fax:* 412-983-5863

Pennsylvania College of Technology
Occupational Therapy Asst. Prgm.
One College Ave.
Williamsport, PA 17701-5799
Tel: 717-326-3761 *Fax:* 717-321-5538
E-mail: bnovell@pct.edu

Puerto Rico

Humacao University College
Occupational Therapy Asst. Prgm.
University of Puerto Rico
CUH Postal Station
Humacao, PR 00791-9998
Tel: 787-850-9390 *Fax:* 787-850-9390

South Carolina

Trident Technical College
Occupational Therapy Asst. Prgm.
P.O. Box 118067
Charleston, SC 29423-8067
Tel: 803-572-6254 *Fax:* 803-569-6585
E-mail: zpstockmaste@trident.tec.sc.us

Greenville Technical College
Occupational Therapy Asst. Prgm.
Greer Campus
506 S. Pleasantburg Dr. P.O. Box 5616
Greenville, SC 29606-5616
Tel: 864-848-2040 *Fax:* 864-848-2038
E-mail: Tessleelt@gutc

South Dakota

Lake Area Technical Institute
Occupational Therapy Asst. Prgm.
230 Eleventh St. NE
Watertown, SD 57201-0730
Tel: 605-882-5284, ext. 326
Fax: 506-882-6347

Tennessee

Roane State Community College
Occupational Therapy Asst. Prgm.
276 Patton Lane
Harriman, TN 37748-5011
Tel: 423-481-3496 *Fax:* 423-483-0441
E-mail: sain_s@a1rscc.cc.tn.us

Nashville State Technical Institute
Occupational Therapy Asst. Prgm.
120 White Bridge Rd./P.O. Box 90285
Nashville, TN 37209-4515
Tel: 615-353-3383 *Fax:* 615-353-3376

Texas

Amarillo College
Occupational Therapy Asst. Prgm.
6222 W. Ninth/P.O. Box 447
Amarillo, TX 79178-0001
Tel: 806-354-6079 *Fax:* 806-354-6076
E-mail: vrgass@actx.edu

Austin Community College
Occupational Therapy Asst. Prgm.
Riverside Campus
1020 Grove Blvd.
Austin, TX 78741-3300
Tel: 512-223-8079 *Fax:* 512-288-8185

Navarro College
Occupational Therapy Asst. Prgm.
3200 W. Seventh Ave.
Corsicana, TX 75110-4818
Tel: 903-874-6501, ext. 367
Fax: 903-874-4636
E-mail: alane@nav.cc.tx.us

North Central Texas College
Occupational Therapy Asst. Prgm.
601 E. Hickory St. Ste. B
Denton, TX 76201-4305
Tel: 940-380-0450 *Fax:* 940-380-0274
E-mail: cmohair@nctc.cc.tx.us

Army Medical Dept. Center and
  School
Occupational Therapy Asst. Prgm.
Bldg. 1447
Ft. Sam Houston, TX 78234-6131
Tel: 210-221-3694 *Fax:* 210-221-4447
E-mail: ltc_valerie_rice@medcom1.
  smtplink.amedd.army. mil

Houston Community College Central
Occupational Therapy Asst. Prgm.
Health Careers Division
3100 Shenandoah
Houston, TX 77021-1098
Tel: 713-718-7392 *Fax:* 713-718-7401

San Jacinto College South
Occupational Therapy Asst. Prgm.
13735 Beamer Rd.
Houston, TX 77098
Tel: 281-922-3467 *Fax:* 281-922-3487
E-mail: jmoes@south.sjcd.cc.tx.us

St. Philip's College
Occupational Therapy Asst. Prgm.
1801 Martin Luther King St.
San Antonio, TX 78203-2098
Tel: 210-531-3416
E-mail: ebeaty@accdvm.accd.edu

Utah

Salt Lake Community College
Occupational Therapy Asst. Prgm.
4600 S. Redwood Rd.
P.O. Box 30808
Salt Lake City, UT 84130-0808
Tel: 801-957-4314 *Fax:* 801-957-4444
E-mail: englanan@slcc.edu

Vermont

Champlain College
Occupational Therapy Asst. Prgm.
163 S. Willard St./P.O. Box 670
Burlington, VT 05402-0670
Tel: 802-865-6491 *Fax:* 802-860-2750
E-mail: lepsic@champlain.edu

Virginia

Southwest Virginia Community
   College
Occupational Therapy Asst. Prgm.
P.O. Box SVCC
Richlands, VA 24641-1510
Tel: 540-964-2555 *Fax:* 540-964-9307
E-mail: annette_proctor@sw.cc.va.us

J. Sargeant Reynolds Community
   College
Occupational Therapy Asst. Prgm.
P.O. Box 85622
Richmond, VA 23285-5622
Tel: 804-786-3484 *Fax:* 804-786-5298
E-mail: srmasok@jsr.cc.va.us

College of Health Sciences
Occupational Therapy Asst. Prgm.
P.O. Box 13186
Roanoke, VA 24016
Tel: 540-985-4097 *Fax:* 540-985-9773
E-mail: ave@health.chs.edu

Washington

Green River Community College
Occupational Therapy Asst. Prgm.
12401 SE 320th St.
Auburn, WA 98002-3699
Tel: 253-833-9111, ext. 4319
Fax: 253-288-3422

Yakima Valley Community College
Occupational Therapy Asst. Prgm.
Sixteenth Ave. and Nob Hill Blvd./P.O.
   Box 1647
Yakima, WA 98907-1647
Tel: 509-574-4951 *Fax:* 509-574-4735
E-mail: pbryant@ctc.ctc.edu

Wisconsin

Fox Valley Technical College
Occupational Therapy Asst. Prgm.
1825 N. Bluemound Dr./P.O. Box 2277
Appleton, WI 54913-2277
Tel: 414-735-4843 *Fax:* 414-735-2582
E-mail: holz@foxvalley.tec.wi.us

Western Wisconsin Technical College
Occupational Therapy Asst. Prgm.
304 Sixth St. N./P.O. Box C-908
LaCrosse, WI 54602-0908
Tel: 608-789-4757 *Fax:* 608-785-9487
E-mail: olson@al.western.tec.wi.us

Madison Area Technical College
Occupational Therapy Asst. Prgm.
211 N. Carroll St.
Madison, WI 53703-2285
Tel: 608-258-2314 *Fax:* 608-258-2480

Milwaukee Area Technical College
Occupational Therapy Asst. Prgm.
700 W. State St.
Milwaukee, WI 53233-1443
Tel: 414-297-7160 *Fax:* 414-297-6851
E-mail: strachoe@milwaukee.tec.wi.us

Wyoming

Casper College
Occupational Therapy Asst. Prgm.
125 College Dr.
Casper, WY 82601
Tel: 307-268-2867 *Fax:* 307-268-2891